Traces of Transcendence

Traces of Transcendence

The Heart of the Spiritual Quest

DUNCAN S. FERGUSON

WIPF & STOCK · Eugene, Oregon

TRACES OF TRANSCENDENCE
The Heart of the Spiritual Quest

Copyright © 2022 Duncan S. Ferguson. All rights reserved. Except for brief quotations in critical publications or reviews, no part of this book may be reproduced in any manner without prior written permission from the publisher. Write: Permissions, Wipf and Stock Publishers, 199 W. 8th Ave., Suite 3, Eugene, OR 97401.

Wipf & Stock
An Imprint of Wipf and Stock Publishers
199 W. 8th Ave., Suite 3
Eugene, OR 97401

www.wipfandstock.com

PAPERBACK ISBN: 978-1-6667-3598-7
HARDCOVER ISBN: 978-1-6667-9372-7
EBOOK ISBN: 978-1-6667-9373-4

02/25/22

Scripture quotations are taken from the New Revised Standard Version Bible, copyright © 1989, Division of Christian Education of the National Council of the Churches of Christ in the United States of America. Used by permission. All rights reserved.

Dedicated to those who search for the truth

The only God who seems to be worth believing in is impossible for mortals to understand, and therefore he teaches us through the impossible. But we rebel against the impossible. I sense a wish in some professional religion-mongers to make God possible, to make him comprehensible to the naked intellect, domesticate him so that he's easy to believe in. Every century the Church makes a fresh attempt to make Christianity acceptable. But an acceptable Christianity is not Christian; a comprehensible God is no more than an idol. I don't want that kind of God.

—Madeline L'Engle

Contents

Preface | ix

    1   Introduction: The Quest for Wholeness and the Rise of Religion | 3

Section One: Ways of Understanding Transcendence in the Premodern World

    2   Extending Outward: The Ways of Nature and History | 21

    3   Opening Inward: The Ways of Meditation and Contemplation | 36

    4   Reaching Upward: The Ways of Faithfulness and Obedience | 49

Section Two: The Modern Quest to Understand and Connect with Transcendence

    5   Creation Spirituality: The Ways of Reason and Reflection | 65

    6   Contemplative Spirituality: The Ways of Introspection and Meditation | 84

    7   Committed Spirituality: The Ways of Obedience and Faithfulness | 104

Section Three: The Current Practices of Spirituality

    8   Compassionate Spirituality: The Ways of Implementing Universal Values | 123

    9   Contemporary Options and Finding a Pathway | 135

Bibliography | 157

Index | 161

Preface

I AM GRATEFUL TO many people—my former teachers, friends and family, and colleagues and authors in the field of religious studies—for the assistance they have given me in the writing of this book. It is their contribution to my education that has given me the confidence to take on the project. I have been taught by good and gifted people, and with their guidance I have been modestly able to work through the complex material that constitutes the content of the book. Further, their influence is present in the way the material is organized and written, and most importantly, in the ways they have nurtured my spiritual growth. Grateful for their guidance and care, my goal is to assist those that are not familiar with the subjects of the book to understand more fully the spiritual dimension of life, the wisdom it offers, and the ways of cultivating it.

I have tried to address this crucial subject with integrity and clarity. For example, in reference to integrity, I have resisted the temptation to cover my lack of knowledge and more generally the human lack of knowledge with my current mindset, preunderstanding, and bias. There is the temptation to simply assert that "it is the way it is" or to insert "that's the way God designed it" when I don't have sufficient information. It is all too easy to use this God-of-the-gaps argument and explanation rather than to offer a well-researched and thoughtful explanation.

Preface

My various friends and teachers have had additional work to do in teaching me how to write more clearly. When I look back on my early writing in the university years, I sense that I have made some progress. I have gone beyond the writing skill that I demonstrated in the first-year university course in writing called English Composition. My professor was gracious and helpful but did not predict that I had found my vocation. I am also grateful to the publishers and editors who have substantially improved my work before it was published.

The subject of the book, traces of transcendence, has emerged as the topic for which I have the most interest and personal investment in writing. I have been engaged for many years in studying the various spiritual pathways of the religions of the human family. As I have visited and observed their sites and cultures and read the foundational writings of these religions, I have gained an appreciation of the many helpful insights and the good measure of wisdom they contain. These insights and wisdom have matured in a deeper and more empathic way in my teaching about these extraordinary human quests. While there is much more to learn, I now sense that I am ready to share some of what I have learned. I thought of many titles, but realized that what I have observed, studied, and experienced could best be summarized by the human quest to incorporate the traces of transcendence into a spiritual pathway.

What I have learned is that human beings, in addition to taking care of the basic concerns of survival and reproduction, have longed for a better understanding of who they are and what they should be doing in life. In many cases, this longing has taken the form of religion, and these religious beliefs and practices have provided understanding and guidance regarding identity and purpose in life. From the most basic religious impulse of our distant ancestors to the most sophisticated expressions of religion in the contemporary world, there has been a spiritual quest to understand whether there is a guiding transcendence (or Transcendence) and what that might be. In many cases, it has been the belief in a personal God and universal ethical norms, as in the three Abrahamic monotheistic religions. There is an "up there," a sense of receiving revelation in this orientation. Great teachers and prophets such as Moses, Jesus, and Muhammad have guided those who had found their way with this orientation. Others have turned to the fundamental principles of order and power in nature and the size and design of our cosmic home and sensed in the natural world an "out there," a transcendent pattern through which one might discern guidance

Preface

in matters of belief and behavior. A similar orientation in the "out there" category is the way that the divine has been sensed in great rulers or government structures such as an empire. Others, drawing upon the great religious traditions of transcendent monism, as in Hinduism and Buddhism, have drawn upon the internal voices of insight and conscience, an "in here" path that leads to the good life. Humans have sought a transcendent reality to help them find direction and peace of mind.

I want to explore this spiritual impulse that is so basic to what it means to be human. In the study, I will seek to describe these spiritual quests, assess their value or lack of it in making life better, and articulate how these quests point to a transcendent reality that stands above, behind, and within them. I will ask whether these quests are simply a human impulse smoldering within us prior to the rise of self-awareness, scientific understanding, and a developed consciousness. Many would argue that they are no more than an impulse, and life's origin and meaning can be much better explained by the patterns of evolution. To this point, I would say, "Yes, there is some truth to this observation, and this simple and basic impulse continues into the present, and it can be explained in rational and scientific ways." But for me, the larger question remains. As these quests have matured, do they point in a more sophisticated and advanced way to an ultimate reality? Do the paintings on the cave wall in France; Buddha's inquiries; the leadership of Moses, which led to liberty and justice; the teaching of Jesus; Muhammad's laws for life; and the dedicated lives of Gandhi and Mother Teresa point to what is foundational and ultimate in terms of understanding our universe and our purpose of life? I suspect they do. This book is about my suspicion; I want to describe how traces of transcendence have developed into mature religious expression, keeping an eye how easy it is to project divine presence into what we do not understand. In short, I want to explore whether we are alone in and simply a product of the evolving universe or whether we might have divine company that is inviting us to a life of inner peace and meaning, empowering us to flourish.

But is progress sustainable? A common response to the good news about our health, wealth, and sustenance is that it cannot continue. As we infest the world with our teeming numbers, guzzle the earth's bounty heedless of its finitude, and foul our nests with pollution and waste, we are hastening an environmental day of reckoning. If overpopulation, resource depletion, and pollution don't finish us off, then climate change will.

—Stephen Pinker

1

Introduction
The Quest for Wholeness and the Rise of Religion

DEFINITIONS AND GOALS

I WANT TO EXPLORE ways to undergird and more fully understand one's belief in God or some other form of transcendence for two primary reasons. The first reason is to find and provide a measure of assurance that the universe has order and purpose and that it is unfolding in a cosmic evolutionary pattern.[1] In general it has an internal logic and consistency, although there are pieces and parts that seem random and uncoordinated. Not all will sense a need for this assurance or even believe that it is attainable. But I gain some peace of mind believing that I live my life in a universe that has order and purpose, guided by transcendence, either a divine creator or orderly powers and principles, or both working in harmony. The second reason is to provide guidance to human beings who believe their creator and sustainer, a personal Transcendence, gives their lives meaning and direction and leads them to maturity, inner peace, and wholeness and health. I want us to find our way in the grand scheme of things, and if we discern where we fit in the grand scheme, we will be better able to discern

---

1. Andrew Cohen, in his book *Evolutionary Enlightenment*, thoughtfully connects spiritual awakening to evolutionary development.

our way in the local situation in which we abide and struggle. We may even survive global warming.

One might ask whether this inquiry is really necessary, and I do acknowledge that it may not be of great value to many people. Food on the table, a glass of wine for dinner, and the children safe in bed may be enough, and in some cases even almost too much. Many people have enough to ponder and worry about in their day-to-day lives, especially at this moment in which I write. I suspect that most of us hope that someone else—perhaps religious leaders, scholars, and scientists—will find some answers to the larger question of where the universe and its small planet called Earth are going and how we might get on course in this direction.

I have come to the tentative conclusion, called *faith*, that if the question is answered truthfully and wisely, it will help us find our way and give us a spiritual pathway in these extraordinarily troubled times. We do need meaning in life and guidance to live out this meaning! If we begin to understand how we fit into the larger scheme of the universe and learn from others who have gone before us, we may be able to discern principles, values, and goals that will save us from what appears to be a disaster, the reality that we are living in ways that harm our home, Earth. We hope to point to ways that help us contribute to creating a more safe, just, and humane world.

The word *transcendence* has several shades of meaning, and I want more closely to define how we will be using the term. We define *Transcendence*[2] as that which creates, stands behind, and, while allowing freedom, guides the flow, patterns, and direction of all of reality. If such a transcendent being exists and we begin to discern the divine intentions of the Transcendent One, we will better understand how to participate in guiding the future of the earth and the place of humankind in this sacred endeavor. This concern often turns toward religion, which takes many forms. I do not want to exclude any of them, but I will tend to use the word *transcendence* primarily as it is understood in the Abrahamic monotheistic religions. It refers to the God who is Love, Truth (Light), and Spirit. Our quest is to get in touch with this personal God who is Love, Truth, and Spirit (omnipresent like the wind), the one that stands behind it all, is engaged with the ebb and flow of all that exists, and invites humankind to connect and link in spiritual and religious ways.

---

2. We use a capital T in this definition, giving it a special meaning, similar to the word *God*. We will not always capitalize it and may use the word elsewhere with related but divergent meanings.

Introduction

In traditional Christian theology, the word *transcendence* is often placed side by side and in slight contrast to *immanence*, with one family of theological persuasion stressing the God who stands behind it all and represents the mystery and the otherness of God, whereas *immanence* describes God as discernable in our day-to-day life, as one who is close, engaged, and accessible.

A brief definition of *religion* in this context is the beliefs and practices that sustain and advance this connection. Generally, a religion has four interwoven dimensions:

1. It has a creed or set of beliefs about ultimate reality.
2. It has a code or a pattern of ethics for the believers to follow.
3. It has a community, a way of gathering together around common beliefs and practices for growth and support.
4. It has a culture, linked to its founding, which expresses its beliefs and practices in a particular time and setting.

We will also use the word *transcendence* in a more generic sense to describe those traces that point to ultimate reality or the way things work in a philosophical and scientific inquiry and understanding. My view is that the two pathways, Transcendence and transcendence, need to integrate, collaborate, and when appropriate include the concept of God's immanence. We need both ultimate meaning and rational and scientific understanding as we seek to clarify our values and heal the earth. I might also mention that on occasion the word *transcendence* may point to preunderstanding, the mindset or prior assumptions we bring to our ways of knowing. As Kant so persuasively argued, we receive knowledge with an outlook that shapes our understanding, that gives it descriptions and meaning that come from within us more than from what we are experiencing or observing.

My aim then in this writing is to gain a better understanding of the human quest for a spiritual center, rooted in transcendence (t & T), one that gives peace of mind, values to guide life, practices that lead to wholeness as a person, and inspiration to serve the common good. I have been on such a quest and have studied many pathways with varying definitions of transcendence and Transcendence that guide one toward wholeness and responsible service. One of my goals in this quest has been to understand with some empathy the many narratives of the human family that suggest a definition of Transcendence, ones that articulate an outlook and way to become a mature and fulfilled human being with a commitment to a life of integrity, compassion, and the quest for justice.

It is been part of my professional responsibility as a teacher in religious studies as well as an honest seeker to study these many views of transcendence and Transcendence that point to spiritual pathways that lead to a good life. I have noted those characteristics that are life-giving, and conversely, suggested those pathways that have elements that are harmful and life-denying.[3] I have been careful to articulate these characteristics, both positive and negative, within the framework of belief systems and the context in which they are manifested. Of course, those that possess these patterns of belief and action have an ever-changing setting with a character and quality that modifies their outlook and guides them in their response to their environment. Cognizant of these constantly changing outlooks, I use the following categories:

Life-Giving Characteristics of Spiritual Pathways:

1. The spiritual pathway *empowers* the person or the group to believe in common goals and practice constructive ways that lead to love, compassion, understanding, and acceptance of those with different guiding narratives.
2. The spiritual pathway *guides* the person or group to be socially responsible and concerned about creating a more just and humane world.
3. The spiritual pathway is *intellectually credible and encourages* the person or the group to be open and responsive to new ideas and challenges. It encourages the quest to find, live, and speak the truth.
4. The spiritual pathway helps the individual to *flourish and integrate* the beliefs and practices into a life of coherence, conviction, serenity, integrity, and service.
5. The spiritual pathway offers guidance and practices that *sustain* the individual and group in times of difficulty and challenge.

---

3. Ferguson, *Spirituality of the World Religions*, 10.

Introduction

Life-Denying Characteristics of Spiritual Pathways:

1. The spiritual pathway is *sectarian* and closed to other religious traditions and points of view. It is cultic, tribal, judgmental, and exclusive.
2. The spiritual pathway is overly *ideological* in character and suspicious of those whose religious beliefs and practices are unlike their own. It is intolerant of difference, it does not account for new ways of understanding reality, and it often lacks intellectual credibility.
3. The spiritual pathway tends to *confine and control* the individuals within the group and asks for blind obedience. It does not liberate, but imprisons.
4. The spiritual pathway is filled with *zealotry* about its way and is inclined to force its way on others, even violently. Often the ends tend to justify the means as religious faith is captured by political ideology.
5. The spiritual pathway inculcates *fear, mistrust, and intolerance* and does not reflect the positive values of personal transformation, compassion, justice, and peace.

It has also been a personal quest to find a way that is filled with life-giving qualities and has few if any of the life-denying characteristics. I have learned that it is a moving target and goal; one does not arrive and relax. I have found that my faith in God and other ways of expressing the reality of transcendence are constantly challenged by emerging new worldviews, by the dramatic changes in our global infrastructure, and by the profound threats to our earth home. Many pastors, priests, and religious leaders whom I know have left their calling, what was for them a vocation, because they no longer believed in or could speak with conviction about their faith tradition. Even suicide has been present among these people. Their religious tradition remained stagnant while they and their understanding of the world had changed.

I judge from these conversations and extensive reading in the field that I am not alone in my need for a thoughtful and contemporary foundation for religious belief and a life-giving spiritual pathway that is responsive to changing realities. In this swirl, there is a vast wave of doubt and struggle.[4]

---

4. There have been other moments in history when the ways of understanding ultimate reality have been challenged and changed, such as the Enlightenment with its emphasis on reason and the rise of scientific understanding, but it does seem intense at

I believe the way forward is to be wise and diligent as we seek the common good and follow it.

Many wise and discerning people who have acknowledged change and sought new ways of understanding reality have inspired and guided me. For example, I have been informed by the writing of Pierre Teilhard de Chardin and others such as Ilia Delio who have sought to integrate faith with scientific understanding. Others such as the Dalai Lama and Thich Nhat Hanh bring love and wisdom to the currently confused and threatening situation in which we live.[5]

THE CHALLENGES

One might ask whether all possible ways to make the case for the existence of God or a transcendent order have already been explored, carefully studied, vigorously reasoned, and then clearly written for all to read and understand.[6] To some extent, this is a valid point; great minds across the centuries have given us their best arguments and explanations that validate our belief in God or a transcendent foundational structure and order and have pointed to ways that would assure a better future. My career as a teacher in the field of religious studies has invited me and even demanded that I study these arguments systematically and review the ways they have been discussed and challenged. This point is especially poignant if I want teach them with the conviction that what they affirm is true.

There are those who will want to maintain that these arguments may be helpful but they really don't prove there is a God or even a modest transcendent order, or provide certainty about where this transcendent other wants us to go or follow, although they may encourage the believer's faith. The heart of this caution, especially in reference to proving the existence of God and knowing the divine will, rests on at least two observations. One is that God is not an object and another presence that exists side by side with other things in the cosmos. God is not just a giant human who is bigger and stronger, and sometimes nicer (although in some traditions not always nicer). God is not an angry judge, a cosmic Santa Claus, or a kind

---

this moment in human history.

5. See Teilhard's several books including *The Phenomenon of Man* and *The Future of Man*.

6. See, for example, Hans Küng's book *Does God Exist: An Answer for Today* and Karen Armstrong's *The Case for God*.

Introduction

grandfather, although children may need some metaphorical comparisons for the beginning of their spiritual journey.

What we mean by the words *God* and *Transcendence* is really something quite different. We are describing a cosmic transcendent other who is ever-present and filled with unlimited love and truth, an eternally present being who is the creator and sustainer of all that exists. God is another order of being (being itself or essence), not just a larger piece of furniture in the universe. God is above it and yet within it and engaged with us in our struggle. Increasingly, to take into account vast changes in worldviews, the word *panentheism* is being used to define our belief, as opposed to traditional theism, in which God is clearly above and beyond with only the occasional visit (e.g., Moses crossing the Red Sea), or pantheism, in which God is described as within the created cosmos, not above and beyond it.[7] Even the language we use to speak about a transcendent other is limited and one must use analogy and metaphor that points to but does not prove the existence of God.

The second observation is that if we understand the Divine to be personal, then our way of *knowing* the Divine is not primarily or exclusively by using logical arguments or scientific proof, although these endeavors may have value and provide a starting place. Our link with God is a relationship cultivated by prayer, meditation, worship, and service. There is partial shift from the left side of the brain to the right side of the brain. We sing and meditate more than we read technical footnotes, maps, and blueprints in our ways of linking with the Divine. We, by faith, connect with a personal God with deep love and loyalty. It is more of an apophatic than a cataphatic approach, although both are present.[8]

I have taken all of this into account as I write about the traces of Transcendence, acknowledging that we are thinking about the Divine in slightly different categories than those used in logic and science, not that we shouldn't use the tools of logic and science. As a young student with a relatively new and unsophisticated faith, I did find the many apologetic treatises arguing for the existence of God persuasive. These views meshed with the presuppositions (and biases) of my new faith, and so it was easy for me to fill in the missing pieces. Now, many decades later, I sense that I

---

7. See Matthew Fox's books *Creation Spirituality* and *Original Blessing*.

8. By *apophatic* we mean that we encounter the Divine by openness and relationship apart from the words of logical reason, and by *cataphatic* (sometimes spelled with a k) we mean that we encounter the Divine and describe this connection more by analogy or symbol, according to a projected image.

must be careful about accepting only those views that fit my mindset and prior understanding. Further, the fact that we are not describing another object in the universe, but the very creator and sustainer of it all, means we must use analogical and metaphorical language that points to God, the "ground of being."[9] Good and careful theological language uses symbol to point to the reality of God and engages in reflecting on a range of traces of the Divine, including the existence of being itself, the experience of bliss and the joy of encounter, and the presence of human consciousness.

I gain some comfort and modest confidence in writing about the traces of transcendence when I know and follow these ground rules. I want to make one other personal observation about my faith journey. The language and concepts we use grow out of our cultural understanding, our time and place in history, and even the language we speak. If we want to make a case for the existence of God, as many others have done, we need to be aware of the lens through which we peer and try to understand the metaphysical assumptions of our historical era. To illustrate this point, we know that we obviously have understood reality largely from the perspective of our culture, language, and historical era. We might also make a slightly more subtle point, one that is increasingly expressed, that all of human existence is on the planet earth, and we understand and affirm truth statements from an earth-centered perspective. It is only on rare occasions that our point of view does expand beyond viewing reality from a tribal, regional, or earth-centered outlook. We have now largely moved to a global view, and perhaps need to expand to a planetary view. Yet in many ways, given what physicists and cosmologists are teaching us, our perspective about reality and transcendence must move in ways that I do not fully understand; it must be intergalactic in character, not exclusively earth-centered, and take into account the new ways of understanding given to us by quantum physics. We are only now learning how to unpack the last four billion years of life or the random patterns of subatomic particles. If God is truly the God of all, then we must begin to peer through advanced telescopes and through contemporary lenses.

---

9. Paul Tillich's thought has been especially helpful in this domain. See his book *The Courage to Be*.

Introduction

GOING FORWARD

With these qualifications in mind, I have gone forward, admittedly with some fear and trembling, and reflected a good deal about what it means to believe that there is a universal ground of being, a sort of superstructure or personal being that stands behind and upholds and guides all of reality. Over the years, this ground of being has been personal and knowable, as in the monotheistic outlook of the Abrahamic monotheistic religions. It has been Christian in my experience, but with great respect for the Hebrew Bible and Judaism and a close watch of Islam in its several expressions. The great Eastern wisdom traditions have taught me so much about the spiritual journey and its practices. The more tribal and oral traditions of native people have taught about respecting and learning from the natural world. Within my Christian frame of reference, I have found the life and teachings of Jesus, as we can know them, to be pivotal in shaping my worldview. What he believed, taught, and did provide me with a good place to start, especially in the way I live my life. It has become more important to me than a metaphysical basis on which I discern ethical guidance. I sense that Jesus got it right in reference to attitudes and behavior.

In all of these traditions, the belief in this *transcendent other* has been religious in nature and functions in such a way that human beings respond in a spiritual and ethical way. Indeed, in these faith orientations there is the deep and profound belief that all that exists is shaped and impacted by the presence of transcendence understood in many different ways. I know that my Christian tradition with its deep belief in a personal and loving God is one major heartbeat of the Abrahamic monotheistic religions. It is one view, yet persuasive and comforting in many ways. These religions and their cousins have postulated the existence of a divine being called God and understand God as creator and sustainer of the universe. While the universe is vast, with earth only a piece of sand on the wide beach of what exists, it is that domain of earth that humans inhabit. The Transcendent One is understood as engaged with the totality of what exists, yet fully present on earth with all that happens here, including human life.

A VARIETY OF CHOICES IN TIMES OF GREAT CHANGE

Transcendence has not always been understood as being centered on a personal and loving God or even in religious ways. Philosophers have often defined and spoken about transcendent principles that stand behind all that exists and should be acknowledged as we seek healthy patterns of life. For example, Plato speaks of universal forms (Ideas) that exist in another realm and underlines the universal and transcendent character of goodness, truth, beauty, and justice. Scientists, especially those interested in cosmology, have sought to discern the origins of the universe and identify structures and laws that are integral to the natural order and its evolution. Noted scientist E. O. Wilson maintains that we can find meaning in life by understanding the natural order and learning from its patterns.[10] Einstein went partway to transcendence with his theories and longed for a more universal calculation that would more thoroughly and accurately explain the universe. His well-known comment "God does not play dice" expresses his view that there is cosmic order. Historians, sociologists, and psychologists point to patterns and structures of the flow of history, the structures and formation of society and culture, and the norms of human growth and development.[11]

I have been interested in all of these disciplines that have described different forms of transcendence, but have focused my attention on the ways that religion at its core has tried to discern the nature of Transcendence and follow its guidance. It is this quest to understand the true nature of ultimate Transcendence or relate to and connect with the ground of being that is the center of the spiritual quest. It is one thing to affirm this reality, but another to understand it and put its principles into practice. What I have observed in my attempt to understand the contemporary practice of religion is that the understanding and definition of the Divine, the transcendent other, *is changing dramatically as it must*. Nearly all of the great religious traditions of the human family have had to adjust their views of Transcendence or the Divine (God) to the place of reason and science and a rapidly changing and threatened world. Only a few small and often isolated religious communities have been able to sustain their traditional patterns of religious belief and practice. Even these groups that have tried to maintain their beliefs and practices have partially accommodated their ways to the changing world around them, often as the result of resisting what they consider to be the threat of the contemporary world to their way of life.

---

10. See his book *The Meaning of Human Existence*.

11. I have found the writing of Ken Wilbur especially helpful in providing a universal frame of reference in which to think and talk about cosmic order and meaning. See, for example, his book *The Religion of Tomorrow: A Vision for the Future of Tomorrow*.

Introduction

A CASE STUDY

I have had the privilege of seeing some of these communities struggle to maintain what they consider to be essential to their true identity and well-being, often expressed in cultural norms and religious practices. I have traveled to over seventy countries and observed this trend, variously expressed. Where it was most evident for me was during the years that we lived in Alaska and visited the rural regions of this vast state. We observed and spoke with Alaska Native people about what they value and want to preserve. Often, with deep regret, these people have had to acknowledge that only a few traditional patterns of life and religious belief have been sustained. Most of the leaders with whom we spoke said that they have largely accepted or at least accommodated to a contemporary and scientific understanding of the world as well as modern social norms and values, in part just to sustain their lives. Modern jets deliver more food than the annual migration of the whales, which now are threatened and protected by law. Most of the populations in these isolated regions are now bilingual, speaking their native language and English, the latter bringing with it contemporary Western culture.

On a much larger scale, nearly every traditional culture has adjusted to the many patterns of change that we all know so well. For example, we all know that there are others who are different from us, those with a different language and culture, and we now live with *diversity*, a diversity that is much beyond that of a neighboring tribe. Many young Alaska Natives have gone outside to complete their education and have returned with numerous ideas about how to change the beliefs and way of life of the Alaska villages. As many of these young Alaska Natives have returned, they have discovered that they have a new way of looking at the world around them, often referred to as a "different" or even a "raised consciousness." They have become aware that better health practices need to be introduced and that the education of children can be improved. Technology can give them much-needed information to improve their lives and the ability to communicate across vast regions. Essentially, they have learned that the standard of living can be raised, especially with the windfall and threat of petroleum products present on the North Slope. When we were there a few decades ago, it was clear that both the Indian and Eskimo cultures were being asked to make changes in a much shorter time than other North Americans, who have had most of the twentieth century to adjust.

Not only were these people asked to make fundamental changes in their behavior in a short period of time, but they also were asked to review their outlook on life, question their ethical values, and rethink their religious heritage and beliefs. If these religious beliefs were exclusively rooted in nature and nature's patterns, those who held these views were asked to see transcendence in different ways, although with great respect for the natural world. Ways of understanding the Divine and the spiritual life were questioned and alternatives were offered. Mission workers had been present in parts of Alaska for a long period of time. The Russian Orthodox tradition had been introduced in the 1700s and other Christian denominations became present in the nineteenth and twentieth centuries. But for many of the Alaska Native people, the presence of new global interests and multiple cultural, ethical, and religious ideas were almost more than they could manage. Some social problems occurred, such as alcohol abuse and dependence on gambling. With the excess of funds from the oil industry, the state did share the wealth with the citizens of Alaska, although these new resources, while welcomed, came fast and adjustments in life became necessary.

Yet adjustments for all of the citizens of Alaska and the rest of the United States became necessary as well. I felt the impact of the dramatic changes occurring in society. I began to realize that in my early commitment to the life of faith my views about God and how to follow God were somewhat naïve. I was grateful that good friends and colleagues helped me to cultivate a more mature understanding. I am still on the trail of challenge and change!

A HISTORICAL MODEL

There is an interesting story in the book of Acts (chapter 17) that describes the apostle Paul's encounter with some Greek philosophers during his missionary travels. He is waiting in Athens for his colleagues to join him. While he waits, he observes and visits the region and begins speaking in a local synagogue. The thoughtful Greeks (Epicurean and Stoic philosophers) who are present wonder if he is speaking about foreign gods as he tells the story of Jesus. They invite him to the Areopagus, a local hill and setting where philosophical ideas were openly honored and discussed, and Paul uses the opportunity to continue his preaching about Jesus. He begins with a description of an alter he has seen and remarks, ". . . I see that in every way you are very religious. For as I walked around and have looked carefully at

Introduction

your objects of worship, I even found an altar with this inscription: TO AN UNKNOWN GOD. Now what you worship is something unknown that I am going to proclaim to you. The God who made the world and everything in it is the Lord of heaven and earth and does not live in temples built by hands" (17:23–24). He goes on to speak about a transcendent God who created humankind and remarks, "For in him we live and move and have our being" and that humans are the offspring of God. The Greek people listening ponder the remarks of Paul, with some believing Paul's message while others remain unconvinced.

I want to note what I think may have been occurring that day when Paul spoke with thoughtful Athenians. There are some lessons for us as we talk about religious ideas.

1. Paul *respected* the Greek culture and their openness to speak with one another and learn from one another. He was a child of this culture, having been born in a neighboring country that is modern day Turkey, and he was a Roman citizen, although his primary beliefs were from Judaism. He wasn't disdainful about what he may have considered their ignorance, but was respectful and used the setting of the Areopagus to share his ideas and observations about Jesus and what had occurred in Jerusalem in the Jesus event.

2. Paul, although I am not sure he was always as pleasant as he appears to have been in this encounter, was *civil and showed empathy and compassion.* He appears to have been willing to enter into their world and consciousness.

3. *A proper setting and respect for others who are different* characterized this encounter. He went to the Areopagus, where different ideas were shared and discussed.

4. *Harsh judgments and provocative language were not present.* There was not an accusation that the people with whom he was speaking were stubbornly ignorant, yet he noted that they had not heard about Jesus, who gave some answers to the implied question at the Altar to the Unknown God. In these kinds of conversations, I have learned how to listen and learn, even if I come with convictions and beliefs that may be different from those with whom I am speaking.

5. Paul stayed in the region for a several days, got acquainted, and *built trust.* In this case, Dionysius, a leader in the programs of the Areopagus,

and a woman named Damaris accepted Paul's teaching about Jesus. Paul *stayed in the conversation and relationship long enough for the formation of a foundation of trust.*

6. The theme of Transcendence, understood in this conversation as God, was *carefully and profoundly discussed.* He left them with several insights about God:

   - We gain our life from God. "In him we live . . ." This is summarized at the end: "We are his offspring," and have, as family members, the image of God.
   - We move and are sustained through life as a gift from God. God is with us through the many stages of life.
   - And our very being is given to us. Who we are, what we value and enjoy, what we believe, and what we do are gifts from God.
   - And, as Paul said that day, God asks us to *repent*, a word frequently associated with God's judgment of our sinful lives and our need to confess and express sorrow. A more precise meaning of the word is that we need to change our thinking and understanding and go in a different direction, rather than to fear an angry God (Acts 17:30).
   - Paul underlined that we do have a choice about how we understand Transcendence, and as we make our choice it becomes a spiritual decision and way of life. It is a gracious invitation. As we hear it and respond, we sense that we get in touch with ultimate reality, gain life-giving insight, deepen our values, and have a new direction in accord with God's will and way. Paul *gave ample time for his listeners and friends to make wise decisions based on thoughtful information.*

I am not saying that Paul had all the answers or that we should accept his message that endorses his teaching about Jesus. We will not necessarily and suddenly have all the truth and know that other ways are wrong. What I am saying is that these people had a civil and thoughtful conversation, listened to each other with respect, and honored those who sought a deep linkage and relationship with Transcendence. Paul spoke about the traces of God within the context of his recent experience and shared with those who had a somewhat different heritage and background.

Introduction

SETTINGS FOR CHANGE AND COMMITMENT

As we explore traces of Transcendence, as did some of the Athenians to whom Paul spoke, we can learn from the content and character of their conversation. We learn that what we do and say should be appropriate and that there is the presence of respect. We also learn that we should talk with others in a civil way as differences are explored. We have empathy and compassion as we listen. We can also make sure that we have provided good information and careful reasoning as together we look more deeply at the several dimensions of change and response that come with conversations about Transcendence.

As I look back at my life at the factors influencing me and the decisions I have made, I discover a very complex landscape, one with similarities to the setting in Athens and the Areopagus. But there were traces of less healthy factors as well, ones that bordered on being tribal and cultic, even exclusive. Neither our limited space nor our purpose allow us to go into great detail about my experience, yet these broad observations have helped me and may help others as we talk and study together about our theme of traces of transcendence.

A primary lesson I have learned is that there may be many pathways to the Divine leading to wholeness, peace of mind, and a life of service. My travels around the world suggest that God speaks many languages and has many faces and descriptions. As we look carefully, we will see signs and symbols that point to Transcendence. In some cases, they take the place of descriptive words that may not be able to capture the subtle and complex dimensions of Transcendence. It is possible for people in different cultures, languages, and religious traditions to be on a path that leads to a good and healthy life. As I study the many religious traditions of the human family, I sense that the main concern is whether the religious community is healthy and offers a pathway that is life-giving. It is also possible that the pathway may be life-denying, leading to fear, harsh judgment, a sectarian spirit, and exclusivity.

As we review the traces of transcendence and as we learn from Paul's experience in Athens, we will be open and eager to learn and grow.[12] In

---

12. There are statements of exclusion, based on belief and practice, in Paul. I prefer to read Paul as remarkably grateful for his transformation and eager to share it dimensions with others. He does so as a faithful mission worker. Yet his views at times may sound to some overly exclusive and sectarian while others find a clear statement the describes the truth.

essence, we are suggesting that there are many ways to understand Transcendence and many healthy spiritual pathways that lead to a mature and healthy life and ways that empower us to flourish. How we believe may be every bit as important as what we believe. Our place in this context is not to so much to change the culture and beliefs of others whose views differ from ours. Rather, it is to help them find ways to move toward wholeness and a flourishing life of love and service.

Section One

Ways of Understanding Transcendence in the Premodern World

For what can be known about God is plain to mankind because God has shown it to them. Ever since the creation of the world, God's eternal power and divine nature, invisible though they are, have been understood and seen through the things God has made.

—THE APOSTLE PAUL, ROMANS 1:19–20a

2

Extending Outward
The Ways of Nature and History

AT SOME RELATIVELY EARLY point in the evolving life of *Homo sapiens* and perhaps of other related hominids, there was, at least in a preliminary way, the emergence of mystery, wonder, and questions.[1] More often than not, the questions, growing out of mystery and wonder, related to the basic needs of these developing human beings rather than the more philosophical questions about life's origins and meaning.[2] They were more inclined to ask how to survive and multiply rather than why they were there and how they should live. The concern was whether they could live in such a primitive setting, not the more philosophical question of whether there was some deeper purpose for life. These questions about meaning have generally

---

1. Condemi and Savatier provide a brief summary paragraph of the emergence and evolutionary development of Homo sapiens in *A Pocket History of Human Development*, 83: "More than 135,000 years ago, the first Sapiens left East Africa to venture into the Arabian Peninsula and into southern parts of Eurasia. They arrived in Australia 65,000 years ago and in China more than 100,000 years ago, and for a long time, multiplied their numbers in these hot climates. Then, stating about 60,000 years ago, after mixing with non-Sapiens populations already present in Eurasia, they began moving farther north entering Europe only 43,000 years ago, and America 20,000 years later."

2. It is likely that there was little or no development of consciousness as yet in this early period.

Section One: Ways of Understanding Transcendence in the Premodern World

been easier for later humans and for those for whom the intrusive demands of life and the threat of death can be kept at a distance.

Discerning how and what these early humans thought is difficult in that they left no written work to express their thoughts. The appearance of some form of writing and literacy is often the key marker in the transition from prehistoric to historic. What we have that gives some clues are scattered remains that suggest rather than fully describe their way of life. It is primarily the work of the paleontologists and archeologists to discern patterns of life from these ancient records that come to us in the form of bones, elementary tools, the occasional object used for defense, pieces of pottery that are related to eating for survival, skins that may have served as clothing, and burial practices. Those of us who seek to understand whether they thought about any form of transcendence have to make difficult judgments in reference to what these archeological remains tell us. We want to pick up only one part of the narrative from these records about how they lived and what they felt, thought, and believed. We want to explore how these ancient clues point to early forms of religious belief and understanding.

A small chart providing the probable dates of trends in human development will give us a context for our inquiry and discussion. Denise L. Carmody and John T. Carmody trace the formation of "the ancient religious mind" in several suggested stages, with the caveat that precise dates for the stages of human development have occasionally been modified as there have been new discoveries.[3]

1. 4.6 billion years ago: Formation of the earth
2. 3.6 billion years ago: Rise of life
3. 4 million years ago: *Australopithecus*: advanced hominid in Africa
4. 2 million years ago: *Homo habilis*: stone tools
5. 1.5 million years ago: *Homo erectus*: more sophisticated tools
6. 500,000 years ago: Use of fire
7. 100,000 years ago: *Homo sapiens*: ritual burial
8. 75,000 years ago: Mousterian cave-dwellers: clothing to survive northern winters
9. 40,000 years ago: More advanced *Homo sapiens*: full hunting culture
10. 35,000 years ago: Clothing adequate for life in Siberia

3. Carmody and Carmody, *Ways to the Center*, 17–18.

Extending Outward

11. 30,000 years ago: Prehistoric painting and sculpture
12. 30,000–025,000 years ago: Migrations across Bering Strait to new world
13. 20,000 years ago: Colonization of Europe and Japan
14. 15,000 years ago: Extensive cereal collecting
15. 10,500 years ago: Humans in most regions of South America
16. 9,500–506,500 years ago: Cereal cultivations and domestication of animals
17. 8000 BCE: Full withdrawal of glaciers
18. 8350–7350 BCE: Jericho: first walled city (ten acres)
19. 6250–5400 BCE: Catal Huyuk (Turkey): large city
20. 6250–5400 BCE: Rice cultivation and woolen textiles
21. 5000 BCE: Irrigation of Mesopotamia and Alluvial Plains
22. 4000 BCE: Bronze carving in Middle East
23. 3500 BCE: Megaliths in Brittany, Iberian Peninsula, British Isles, and invention of the wheel
24. 3100 BCE: Pictographic writing in Sumer
25. 3000 BCE: Spread of copper-working

THE CONNECTION BETWEEN NATURE AND RELIGION

As one reviews these dates and the essential development and characteristics of the time periods, one discovers that there was an early rise of religious thoughts, feelings, and practices. Perhaps the best clues we have come from the obvious needs of these early humans or *Homo sapiens*, emerging as a more advanced hominid about 100,000 years ago. However, there were other hominids, perhaps as many as six or more, likely migrating from Africa to the Mid-East, parts of Asia, and Europe. Gradually, several developments enabled *Homo sapiens* to advance their hominization, including their larger brains, bipedalism, the development of the hand, and cultural transmission (passing on basic skills and utilizing some forms of collaboration).[4] Most fundamental of the needs of these early humans was

4. Condemi and Savatier, *Pocket History of Evolution*, 17–25.

Section One: Ways of Understanding Transcendence in the Premodern World

food and security for survival, the need to reproduce in order to continue the family, and to advance into small groups, hordes, and in time tribes.

We do know that these early humans were scattered, living in small groups, some of which functioned as an early form of tribe.[5] In addition to the needs of survival and reproduction, there were the needs for clear roles and responsibilities for members of the groups, some to serve as warriors to protect the group, some to hunt and gather food, and others to prepare food and to care for children. Inevitably there was a need to clarify roles and to determine how to make decisions, how to manage conflicts, and where to locate in order to survive and even thrive.

From this array of concerns and needs, there was a deep awareness that there were *forces in nature* that were powerful and full of components and characteristics that were obviously protective and sustaining while others were profoundly threatening. Nature was in many ways viewed as transcendent and often personified, and there was a strong tendency to fear nature's ambivalent ways while also being grateful to nature because it gave and sustained life.

One fundamental question for them was how to collaborate and cooperate with the forces of nature and get them on their side. In many cases, this impulse was religious in character. From nature came food, patterns of weather, and seasons of time; it was a force that acted upon them and over which these early humans had little or no control. For example, there were storms that impacted their access to food and shelter, and later in this prehistorical period it shaped the early forms of agriculture. There were the changing seasons, with punishing weather that went from freezing temperatures to intense heat. A variety of animals were present with which they shared a domain and habitat. The animals, along with the weather, were a blessing as well as a curse. They were a source of much-needed food, but they had to be hunted and in many cases were very dangerous. In addition, there was fire for light, and as it became more controlled, it gave them warmth and a means for cooking food.

There was a religious impulse, growing as it often does out of fear of the unknown, to try to live in harmony with the rhythms of nature. Out of these endeavors and experiences there arose an early form of religion, one that in time became a pattern of beliefs and practices. One common form was the beginning of what one might describe as a form of worship, both individual and corporate. It was a time when nature and its powerful manifestations

---

5. Condemi and Savatier, *Pocket History of Evolution*, 99–114.

were feared, honored, and praised. At times, attempts were made to appease nature's apparent anger expressed in thunder, lightning, and extreme and changing temperatures that caused deep fear and the loss of life.

Individual components of nature were given divine and transcendent status. The sun was worshipped as it gave light and heat (as did fire); the moon, perhaps a step down on the pantheon, allowed movement at night; and the wind, an ever-present expression of divinity, both warmed and chilled. At other times there were attempts to make sacrifices to gain nature's favor. Gifts were given to honor nature's power and food was given to feed the spirits of those who had died and lived in a shadowy purgatory, a netherworld. Animal sacrifices, and perhaps even violence toward others and human sacrifice, were given to appease the unknown divinity's punishing ways. Sacrifices of animals were made to atone for misdeeds, often a violation of *taboos* that were thought to be against the wishes of these gods of nature.

Early in this period, there were those in the tribe or group that were singled out as having wisdom and divine access. The *shaman*, a person sanctioned by the community to exercise powers to control spirits, was called upon to appease nature, guide religious practices, and offer wisdom.

This complex pattern of nature, often circling from life to death, became the central component of prehistoric religion. With a life span of less than half of ours, death came more frequently and became a regular intruder on the dimensions and patterns of prehistoric life. There were prayers offered to this omnipresent force of nature, prayers for expectant mothers, prayers to control the weather to insure food, prayers for healing, and prayers for protection from hostile neighbors. In ancient caves, there are remains that suggest that there was an effort to make contact with the natural forces that had so much power. Stories were told about great warriors, and dances were made to mimic the gait of the bear, the size and danger of the mammoth, and the leap and grace of the tiger. Some of these practices and dances are preserved in a few isolated cultures. Statues (megaliths) were erected to honor the dead, and great stones were arranged to pattern the sunrise and sunset in different seasons. Perhaps best known is the case of Stonehenge, located in Great Britain, where prehistoric peoples attempted to pattern the movement of the sun and make contact with the transcendence of nature. In many cases, the most powerful elements in nature were personified, praised and feared, often held dear, and even worshipped.

Section One: Ways of Understanding Transcendence in the Premodern World

THE RELIGIONS OF PRELITERATE PEOPLE

Over the centuries of this early period of human development, religion, both its beliefs and its practices, became a way to tame, navigate, and honor the powerful forces of nature. In some cases, as these forces were personified, religion took the form of worship, with ways to praise the "gods" of nature, gain some of the power of nature, appease its destructive side, and obtain forgiveness for deeds offensive to these gods. Increasingly, belief in transcendence became an integral dimension of the life of the people. A brief review of some of these religious beliefs and practices will illustrate how these broad tendencies became specific in a particular time and place. As we turn to these religions, we should note that nature has continued across the span of human presence on earth as a major theme in religion and more directly in spirituality.[6]

THE PLACE OF TRANSCENDENCE IN THE CULTURES OF PREHISTORIC AMERICAN INDIANS AND ESKIMOS

As we have noted regarding the cultures of the American Indians and Eskimos in Alaska, these peoples have had to make a huge leap to feel comfortable in contemporary America. Many, of course, have fully endorsed the current culture and made their adjustments. Yet even with these adjustments to contemporary American life, there is a minority of the American Indian and Eskimo peoples that have made only a partial adjustment and have attempted to preserve their heritage. Even those who have fully entered into the customs and values of American life have found ways of partially preserving their heritage just as others in our nation of immigrants have preserved their unique heritage. I am fully American in my outlook (although not always comfortable with our ways and values) yet still honor my Scottish roots. I lived in Scotland for approximately three years, did my doctoral studies at the University of Edinburgh, and I continue to visit Scotland and enjoy tracing my heritage.

While living in Alaska and for many years in the Pacific Northwest, I have been exposed to both the Eskimo and Indian cultures. What I have

---

6. We will say more about this subject, but at this point I want to call attention to a current author whose books give nature a primary place in the cultivation of a deeper spirituality. See Belden C. Lane's *Backpacking with the Saints: Wilderness Hiking as Spiritual Practice* and *The Great Conversation: Nature and the Care of the Soul*.

Extending Outward

learned from this exposure, primarily in North America rather than in Central and South America, is that these people have preserved many of the beliefs and practices of their heritage, ones that have deep roots in nature. Each tribe and tradition has certain distinctive features, yet they also have much in common.[7] I want to focus on five of these common elements, which provide a perspective on the way the natural world shaped their religious life.

1. Central to many religious traditions, there is a way that the *Divine* (God or Transcendence) is understood, often rooted in prehistoric times.[8] In the case of the North American Indian and Eskimo cultures as well as other native peoples, the terms for god and nature were almost synonymous, especially as elements and creatures of nature were given divine status. The sea and the sky, vast and wild, pointed beyond and took on a transcendent identity. They could not be controlled or changed and remained a transcendent presence in their common life. The creatures of nature represented certain features of divinity, such as grace and beauty, nourishment, and danger. In Northern Alaska, the whale was central for food and survival as it came and went in harmony with the changing patterns of summer and winter. These expressions of divinity were not philosophical in character, but the subjects of story and dance, ways of living in harmony with the Divine and gaining divine approval and blessing. Hunters ventured into the unknown to gather food, and as they did they sensed the presence of transcendence as they explored the wilds with its allure and danger. Inspired by religious belief, they ventured into the natural world around them with both courage and a good measure of respect and fear.

2. As they returned, bringing sustenance and stories, *ceremonies and rituals* developed, some that were positive and filled with gratitude and others that were somewhat negative in that they represented the fear of being rejected and punished by the sacred power. Of course, some of the warriors did not return, and they were mourned and honored as great heroes in ceremonies and dances. These events were a form of ritual protection, a sort prayer dance asking for safety, nourishment,

---

7. There is an abundance of well-researched and thoughtful literature describing the cultures of both the American Indian and Eskimo.

8. I am aware that some of the great religions of the world focus more on personal transformation (Buddhism, Taoism, etc.) than on a personal God as understood in monotheism.

and fertility. Some of the North American Indians began to think about a universal spirit that might bless the hunting endeavors. This concept of spirit developed and became a notion akin to the monotheistic notion of God and was called the *Supreme Spirit*. One distinctive ritual was the way they asked male adolescents to participate in a vision quest; it was a rite of passage and a time for training for the anticipated move toward maturity. As part of their preparation, there would be a steam bath in which the young would be blessed, and then they were sent out to venture alone into the wilderness to learn about the dangers of their terrain and the risks associated with hunting.

3. In many of these religious expressions, there is the notion that human beings should live in such a way that they will be rewarded in some form of *eternal life*. In the Indian and Eskimo cultures of North America, this notion was present although not central. The emphasis was on living in the present and having integrity with the values of the tribal religion. As there were ideas about another life after death, these ideas were often described in terms of the natural world. For example, the Pueblos believed that they might become rain clouds when they died and nourish the land. The Hopi buried dead infants in fertile soil with the hope that their souls might return in future children. It was not uncommon for these tribes to think and to speak about a form of reincarnation, much like the recurring patterns of nature.

4. Still another dimension of the religion of the North American Indians and Eskimos was the emergence of a person in the tribe that would be gifted with spiritual wisdom and help the tribe navigate the wonders and dangers of nature. The community sanctioned this person, called a *shaman*, to exercise some control over the influence of spirits. They also were thought to have the gift of divination or connecting and communicating with the gods and the spirits of the dead. In addition, they were essential to the tribe as they used their power for healing. They were a vital and integral part of the religious communities of the native traditions of North American, and indeed many of the prehistoric tribes in other parts of the world.

5. I want to mention one other dimension of the religions of early North America, one that has been suggested yet needs more development. It is the notion that it is possible for humans to act in such a way that they incur the wrath and punishment of the gods (various forms of

Extending Outward

transcendence). These actions are called *taboo*, which may be defined as a prohibition against a certain action such as eating a prohibited food, going to a forbidden destination, or violating a sacred rule. If one engages in a taboo or forbidden action, it may cause the anger of the gods or spirits, and perhaps the person will find that they have been punished in the form of an illness or some other form of suffering.

THE PLACE OF TRANSCENDENCE IN THE CULTURES OF THE PREHISTORIC PEOPLE IN AFRICA AND AUSTRALIA

Many of the features of the religious life of the preliterate peoples of North American were also present in the cultures of the prehistoric people of Africa and Australia. In fact, the cultures in these regions of the world developed earlier than those of the Americas. The *Homo sapien*, as a slightly more advanced hominid, was perhaps the first to begin acknowledging the presence of some form of transcendence.[9] As we look briefly at the preliterate people of Africa and Australia, we discover five additional components of the early religious life and mind of humankind.

1. These pre-historic people began to do some reflection about how the world works, and these reflections took the form of *myth*, a sacred story that captures a profound moral or sacred truth. It often contained the story of creation, such as the description of creation in the book of Genesis. Myth, in this case, should not be understood as just a superstition that is not true, but a prehistoric way of expressing a profound truth as good stories often do. In fact, the stories we have among the early people of Africa and Australia, as they were told and pondered, might be called a *worldview*. For example, traditional African religion often began with a belief in a supreme being, a transcendent spirit that is far away, but still engaged in the lives of these early people. The engagement with human life, not unlike the transcendence of the early North American people, had subordinate powers that were essentially rooted in nature, such as the spirits of the weather, the wind and storm, the role of water, and trees providing material for crafts. For example, in the hymn to Mwari, the god of the Mashona of

---

9. See Condemi and Savatier, *Pocket History of Human Evolution*, 69–82, in which the authors speak about culture as the evolutionary accelerator and stressing the bigger brain of *Homo sapiens* as providing the reasoning power to advance human development.

southern Zimbabwe piles rocks into mountains and sews the heavens like cloth to protect the people from storms.[10] In many ways, the early African people looked upon nature as more of a blessing, a transcendent power that provides what one needs for the good and safe life, rather than a force to be feared, which was more common among the prehistoric people of North America.

2. One form of this blessing was the way they saw nature as providing all one needs in life. Nature also gives special treasures, beyond basic needs, as one looks closely. While the Africans did not use the term, one thinks of the Polynesian term *manna* as an integral component of nature's gifts. *Places, certain foods, and objects became sacred.* There was a belief in a vital force that animates all of nature, and this vital force is present in special ways, in people, actions, places, and objects, to improve the life of humans. Nature is bountiful and gives life, and provides food to sustain life, material for shelter, and the sexual relationship for reproduction. For them, sex was pleasurable and natural, and it was less feared and controlled by prohibitions than in other cultures. Often it had a sacred quality.

3. In the early religious life of the peoples of both Africa and Australia, there was the strong sense that the *souls of ancestors* continue to be present and take an active interest in the present generation. It was believed that they are capable of both great good, helping the descendants, and great harm if they are displeased. Offerings such as food were made to these ancestors. This belief was quite strong among Aboriginal Australians. The Europeans, when they arrived in Australia, did not fully understand why these people were somewhat passive about present life and its challenges. The people whom the Europeans met seemed to live in a different time frame, insensitive to the seasons. In their religious services, they appeared to enter into the dream-time of the eternal ancestors, believing it to be the real time of the world. To these people, the Europeans seemed to be overly anxious and preoccupied with the present, not acquainted with real time that includes ancestors. Dreams were as much part of reality as the hours and days or normal life.

4. Another dimension of the religion of prehistoric Australians was the special place given to items that represented the spirits of their

10. Carmody and Carmody, *Ways to the Center*, 40.

ancestors. Called *totems*, these sacred objects were often plants, animals, or wooden carvings that represented the emblem of the family or clan, and they called to mind the ancestors who were the founders of the clan. The totem was a symbol of remembrance and a reminder that the ancestors were just below the surface of the earth, but could be called upon for wisdom, guidance, and protection.

5. In general, it should be noted that the world of prehistoric peoples was not driven by a scientific understanding of the world, but by what is often called *divination*, a special gift of the shaman or medicine *man*,[11] a diviner who sees below the surface and beyond objects of daily life and possesses divine insight and wisdom. This person is one who has a spirit that is able to read omens, is able to interpret the movement of sacred animals, is in touch with ancestors, and is able to heal. Often this person would point to a supreme being who controls all of reality and has a sacred plan or scheme for the universe. The role of the diviner or shaman is to follow and explain this cosmic design.

COMMON THEMES AND PRACTICES

There was great diversity among the prehistoric and preliterate peoples of the ancient world, with each region having distinctive features. Yet there are some common elements. I want to underline several of these shared components of the religious mind of these peoples and explore what dimensions of their beliefs and practices might suggest a way of affirming a transcendent reality. It is important to note that these beliefs and practices lacked the subtlety and sophistication of contemporary religious thought and practice. Yet their simplicity and direct emotional expression may suggest a kind of integrity that is lacking in the religious life of the modern world. As we define, analyze, and debate about the range of beliefs in contemporary religious life, we may have lost some of the pure joy and inner peace that comes from too much analysis and not enough direct experience.

We celebrate the rise of human consciousness, but know that an overly cerebral approach may move us away from a direct encounter with Transcendence. Over the years I have been in many small groups seeking a deeper spirituality, and not infrequently as I make an observation I am gently reminded that there are other times and places for careful scholarship

11. Women too had special gifts of discernment and wisdom.

Section One: Ways of Understanding Transcendence in the Premodern World

and analysis. I often point out that direct experience and careful scholarship are not mutually exclusive. Those in the group acknowledge this valid observation, but ask that I please honor what they are doing now, making contact with the Divine and sustaining a relationship. There is the deep need to be present to the stillness of the moment and, through a form of meditation, enable the ego to die before the wild beauty of nature. One must learn how to live in the eternal now, often easier in the quiet beauty of nature.

The common element in the developing religious life and thought of these ancient people is the theme of this chapter; they shared a deep reverence for and experienced some fear of the *grandeur of nature*. They came into the world in a natural way, were raised in the context of the wild, and learned how to navigate in the ever-changing, powerful, and omnipresent natural order. As creatures of nature, they soon learned how to live and survive in nature. They lived in the shade of trees and were protected by nature's ways in caves. They were clothed in the skins of wild animals, found food in the forest and the lakes, and knew that survival depended on the ways they stayed safe and reasonably comfortable from nature's heat, cold, thunder, lightning, rain, and snow. Often, they would have to move in order to find a new setting, free from the threat of threatening tribes, with tolerable weather and access to food.

My wife and I, in our early years, when careers influenced our location, often talked about living in a setting that would allow us to experience and appreciate the beauty and grandeur of nature. In retirement, we have chosen the Pacific Northwest, a sort of return home for us in that we were born there, but more importantly a place of beauty where the mountains, the rivers, the lakes, and the ocean are just a short ride away and partially visibly from our windshield. It has allowed us to experience the power and beauty of nature in a very direct way; as we cross on the ferry on our way home, we may see a whale or seal, and on clear days we look at the islands and the mountains and sense a measure of joy and peace. Even more directly, we encounter nature in our walks in the wild and sense that somehow we are children of nature.[12]

These experiences remind us of a second component of the religious thought and experience of the ancient people. It is that they had *great courage in and trust of nature*. It was not where they went on vacation or where they moved at retirement, but an ever-present reality. When I venture into

---

12. We have moved from the region of the Puget Sound to the forests and lakes of Central Oregon.

the wilderness, I follow a trail prepared by a thoughtful and knowledgeable ranger, read directional signs, and after of few hours of hiking head back to the car and drive home to our warm and comfortable house (largely made from the resources of nature). It has not been common, nor do we expect it to be, that our trek into the center of the forest is dangerous, filled with poisonous plants, wild animals, and threatening warriors from another tribe. Our distant ancestors were intimately connected to nature and its blessings, but also had to deal directly with constant danger. Not infrequently they encountered what they did not expect, threatening weather and dangerous animals that attack and then get away because nature has given them the gifts of smell, hearing, speed, and the ability to hide from that which threatens them. Inevitably, these early humans faced disillusionment because they often encountered what they did not expect and came back to their modest camp with little food and perhaps a serious injury. In addition, they aged much earlier than we do, and death was a common guest in their lives. Eternal night came early for them. Yet they did not easily give up, began to discern the ways of nature, and continued their way of life as one of nature's most advanced creatures. Around the fire, they felt the majesty of nature.

 It was often around the fire that a third common religious feature of these ancient people was visible. It was the feeling of *being centered within a common frame of reference*. It may have been a time of a certain kind of innocent mindfulness with a focus on the present moment and awareness of what was going on inside of them. Perhaps there was reflection and conversation about the beauties and challenges of nature with the result that common goals were achieved that improved the life of the family and tribe.

 I have been quite conscious over these past few years of the ways that I have failed to live in the present and spend uninterrupted time in nature, and have missed its joys and enrichment. My restless monkey mind has often taken over, and instead of celebrating the beauties and joys of the present moment, I have become focused on the past, with feelings of guilt and regret. I have often felt controlled by my guilt, wondering why I had acted in such a careless, even harmful way. I have wondered how to become more mature and have deeply wanted to become a person with integrity. As these feelings have subsided, I have gone directly to the future, feeling insecure with my resources and support systems and anxious about my ability to manage future challenges. As I have pondered all of this, my ego has needed to take over and I have begun to explore ways to gain approval and praise from those around me, especially from those who have made

Section One: Ways of Understanding Transcendence in the Premodern World

me feel insecure and less worthy. In general, instead of enjoying a peaceful present, I have asked whether there would be enough money to pay for the way of life we have chosen and enough friends and family to give me a sense of belonging and support.

These feelings have come and gone, of course, but increasingly I have begun to be kinder to myself, aware that I have some gifts and that I am essentially an ethical person. This has led to a life filled with more awareness of the beauty and goodness that surrounds me. I have become more attentive to my present life, intentional about acting from my internal moral compass (provided by my faith orientation), and listening to my body through my breathing, and caring for my health by the way I eat, the way I exercise, the way I get rest, and the way I sense the Divine within. And, perhaps most importantly, I have been kinder to those around me, and have learned about living the love that I had taught in the church and university classes. Becoming more mindful and more loving has been a great blessing.[13]

These early people did not likely have the benefit of more advanced self-awareness, a moral code that invited them to be caring and compassionate, and an understanding of the complexity of life, the world, and the cosmos. But perhaps they were more centered and focused and lived in the present. Yet, in their immediate circumstances, they had what is another and a third common dimension of the religious mind and spirit of these ancient people. It was the *omnipresence of fear because they were surrounded by danger*. The omnipresence of fear entered into their religious life, and they hoped that their religious beliefs and practices might give them *at least a partial capacity to devise ways to deal with its many expressions and consequences*. The presence of fear is addressed in nearly all religious thought and community life.

Ways to manage failure, guilt, and fear became a common element in the religious mind and spirit of these preliterate and prehistoric people. They understood the transcendent or divine as providing the way to manage these complex emotions. They did so by naming them and taming them, and by being aware of danger and arranging community life in a way that protected people from threatening weather, lack of food, attacks of neighboring tribes, and internal conflict. Their religious practices dealt with these dangers that surrounded them. The common protective elements were:

---

13. Writing the books *Lovescapes: Mapping the Geography of Love* and *Mindful Spirituality* was a helpful endeavor.

- a set of beliefs or *creed* that helped them understand their environment and their own tendencies to harm others;
- a pattern of behavior or *code* of ethics that encouraged the safety of all of the people and the common good of the tribe;
- a supportive *community* that offered belonging, guidance, understanding, forgiveness, comfort, and support; and assured them of a place to live, to sleep with some comfort and to have sufficient food;
- a common *culture* that provided a common understanding of life, ethical norms, shared patterns of behavior, a common language an identity and sense of belonging, and the assurance that what they believed and did was appropriate.

Many of these patterns of religious life among these early people were also present in other parts of the world. Because of differences in time and place, culture and language, climate and soil, and evolutionary heritage, religion took a different form among the peoples of Asia. It is to these patterns we now turn in order to understand better other traces of transcendence.

3

Opening Inward
The Ways of Meditation and Contemplation

NATURE HAS HAD A sacred place in nearly all of the great religions of humankind, especially in their early development. Through nature—its beauty, its dangers, and its power—the people of the world have found traces of transcendence and Transcendence. It was certainly the case in the early development of religious thought and practice in the Americas, Africa, and Australia. It was present as well in the development of the religious life of the peoples of the Middle East, South Asia, and East Asia. Nature had a vital role to play in the religions of these regions, although a more mystical and devotional outlook was more central in the formation of religious thought and practice in the East. While the peoples of the Americas, Africa, and Australia certainly looked inward and reflected on their internal experience, they were more apt to look outward to the forces of nature to form and understand their religious feelings and shape their religious thoughts. At the risk of some oversimplification, we might say that the people the Middle East, South Asia, and East Asia tended to open and look primarily inward to form their religious ideas and practices. Contemplation and meditation were the means of making contact with the Divine. They sensed that there were universal principles that were integral to this deeper truth that could lead to a life of meaning, inner peace, and purpose. These religions are often called *transcendental monism* in that they sought that

Opening Inward

singular reality within that gave them a sense of purpose and guidance in life and awakened them to a deeper reality or Presence. To quote from the Upanishads, "I give you another thousand cows! Please teach me more of the way of self-realization."[1] As if to say, "Sacred cows may be important, but finding that one deep inner truth, awakening to it, and becoming a whole person have more value."

These tendencies to sense transcendence often reflect and are defined by the particular character and challenges of the historical era in which they developed. For example, very early humans lived with the challenges of their external environment; it was their natural habitat and was the focus of their attention. From it came religious ideas that were expressions of how to live with nature's challenges. Somewhat later in history, with the challenges of nature more under control, there was an expansion of human consciousness shaping the development of religious thought. We see the emergence of religious ideas that are more introspective and oriented toward contemplation and meditation. The challenges of nature were still present, yet forms of wonder and mystery about all that they faced emerged. From this reflection came elements of wisdom and enlightenment that went beyond mere survival.

As we look carefully at the development of the religious mind in different times and places, we sense that one way these religious viewpoints may be identified and described is by directional and metaphorical patterns: *extending outward* to nature and sensing power in the Divine, *opening inward* through contemplation for wisdom and enlightenment, and then *reaching upward* toward the Divine for guidance and healing. These trends may be traced to evolutionary development, as hominids developed self-awareness and consciousness. On the collective level, as hordes became more organized tribes, we see diversified roles for members of the tribe. In time, there was the beginning and formation of larger groups and the birth and early forms of what might be called *cities* and *states*. All of this is another story, but it impacts the development and formation of religious thought and practice: religion has individual components, but tends to be a tribal and a community endeavor.

We need to acknowledge once again that a strong case can be made that religious beliefs and practices can be explained on one level by the physical and social sciences. The case can be made that one does not really need the additional dimension of Transcendence for an explanation of the

---

1. Easwaran, trans., *Upanishads*, 112.

dramatic changes that took place. Yet, for many, the big question still remains: does an evolutionary and social science explanation of religious life fully explain it, or do we need a reference point of Transcendence or some other overarching principle to capture the essence of religion and meaning in life? For example, do we need both the sciences and theology for an enlightened understanding of human development? Harvard psychology professor and noted author Steven Pinker as well as many other scholars are clear that we do not need theology with its presupposition of God except to better understand what we are rejecting. Religious studies only provide one form of interpretation about the way things happen in the natural flow of human life, but do not point necessarily to the design of a divine architect. He writes: "Can we really have good without God? Has the godless universe advanced by humanistic scientists been undermined by the findings of science itself? And is there an innate adaption to the divine presence—a God gene in our DNA, a God module in the brain—which ensures that that theistic religion will always push back against secular humanism?"[2] He goes on to say that we have can have much that is good without God; the sciences can give us a full understanding of human development, including human self-awareness, a sense of meaning, and moral sensitivity. A theologian might respond by saying that these human traits cannot be explained as an accident of cause and effect, but point to Transcendence.

I am reminded of a panel discussion that I attended several years ago that included a clergyperson, a lawyer, and a member of the city police. The topic was: "How Do We Understand the Recent Automobile Accident in which Three People Were Killed?" The subject might just as well have been about a recent earthquake or forest fire that caused death and suffering. The police person led off with a description of the accident, the slick road, and the failure of one driver to stop quickly enough at the change to a red light. He noted that those responsible in his domain would likely arrest the driver who went through the red light and make sure that the intersection would be safer with a few modest changes. The lawyer went on to say that the driver who went through the red light was at fault and that the families of the persons who were killed would probably sue the driver and expect major compensation. The clergyperson was asked why this happened and whether there was any divine transcendence behind this terrible death. Why did God let it happen and how would a religious outlook bring comfort to those who were suffering because of the accident?

2. Pinker, *Enlightenment Now*, 420.

Some wise answers were given, but the majority of the people said that the religious answers were unnecessary. The accident just happened because people were careless and the intersection was a bit dangerous. In the future, let's be more careful and fix the intersection.

As one expands this occurrence on an earth-wide frame and introduces climate change and global hunger onto the screen, the questions remain somewhat the same. Is there any transcendence or Transcendence integral and related to all of this danger and suffering, and is there a way through God's power and grace to solve these problems and bring understanding and comfort to those who suffer? I am maintaining that people across the ages have looked for traces of Transcendence in good and bad circumstances. For those of us with a religious orientation do wonder if the police and the lawyers and perhaps politicians need another reference point in order to be motivated to act justly and compassionately and be given wisdom about what should be done to improve the common good. Yet the contemporary vote in these situations would probably say that good police, wise lawyers, and honest government officials should be able to handle it. We need the transcendence of good laws and infrastructure, but not Transcendence, Source, or Presence. The clergyperson would likely say that they need a way for their conscience to be sensitized to human suffering and their attitudes and spirit need the transcendent presence of the root values of compassion and justice.

This very question came up in a story from the Holocaust about a Jewish woman refugee in Germany during the Second World War. She was forced out of her home, was vulnerable and oppressed, and as she walked alone in the freezing weather she was taken in by a Christian pastor and his family, fed and clothed, and given a safe home. When the story was retold, reference was made to the words of the Jewish man from Galilee:

> I was naked and you gave me clothes,
> I was hungry and you fed me,
> I was thirsty and you gave me a drink,
> I was homeless and you gave me a room,
> I was shivering and I was sick and you stopped to visit,
> I was in prison, and you came to me. (Matt 25:35–36)

The pastor went on to say: "Whoever does not love God will always be dividing humans into races, classes, or other kinds of groups. We, on the other hand, know that God abides in the soul of every human being. Every human can find God there and can hear God's voice. Every human possesses

Section One: Ways of Understanding Transcendence in the Premodern World

the capacity to look within, where God can always be revealed. Sometimes this happens without us being aware of it. God's love teaches us how we to are to love . . . Every human is a bearer of God's image in the world."[3]

A touching story does not prove that there is a loving God and an ultimate source of wisdom and guide for behavior. But it does suggest that the human family has for centuries looked within (opened inward) to find Transcendence and discovered that love is the ethical center of life.[4] Several religions of the human family, while sensing transcendence in many ways and domains, have looked inward through prayer, meditation, and contemplation to find wisdom, guidance, and empowerment. They have maintained that through these beliefs and practices, as one opens inward, one will find their true identity, wisdom and knowledge, and a life of meaning, purpose, and inner peace.

PREMODERN HINDUISM

Hinduism is a religious tradition that has consistently encouraged the practice of turning inward to awaken and to find knowledge, wisdom, insight, and inspiration to sustain a healthy and productive life and a social context that is just and peaceful. It had its origins in the north of India in Persia. With the migrations to India of the Aryan people of Persia (1900–1600 BCE), the practices of the emerging religious beliefs and practices in India began to reflect the ideas of these immigrants. This new religious orientation was called Hinduism, a word similar to and meaning India; it meant essentially the beliefs and practices of the people of India. These beliefs and practices were diverse, connected in many ways to the culture and languages of the tribal character of India in its early development. There was an assortment of components in this early period, for example, the power of a shaman, the use of totems, the presence of taboos, and sacrifices of various kinds. Suffering, disease, and death were addressed in their religious practices. It was into this context that the developing beliefs of the new religious movement began to take shape, reflect the Indian context, and address the needs, concerns, and the indigenous religious practices of the people of India.[5]

3. Schott, *Love in a Time of Hate*, 10, 14.
4. See Bishop Michael Curry's book *Love Is the Way: Holding On to Hope in Troubling Times*.
5. See the excellent brief history of Hinduism entitled *A Short History of Hinduism*,

Opening Inward

In its earliest form, this new religion was shaped by the agriculture that was central to the welfare of the Indian people. Nature at that time had a significant role in shaping religious understanding and practice. It was a farming country and the people used religious categories to describe the need for divine help to maintain their crops with adequate water and to increase fertility. India, even with the invasion of the Aryan people, remained somewhat isolated because of its geography; it was protected and isolated by its border of high mountains and river valleys. This meant that Hinduism developed primarily by these new Persian ideas and their interaction with the existing culture and context of India.

Hinduism is a very complex religion and has evolved over many centuries. Our goal at this point is not to fully describe its many dimensions and expressions in contemporary India and its spread worldwide. Our goal is rather to look briefly at its founding ideas that spread widely in premodern India. As is the case in most developing cultures, these new ways of understanding did not produce a way of religious life and set of beliefs that were comprehensive, systematic, and orderly. I wrote in an earlier book that Hinduism has *accents* and *patterns* that fit different places and times in the vast region of India.⁶ It has a wide range of beliefs and practices reflecting different regions and the challenges of the people at certain periods of time. For example, there is the accent of many gods (called *devas*) to worship, which have the power to help with the changes and challenges of human life. These gods tend to be local and regional and are religious expressions of the need to staying alive and deal with climate, disease, hunger, and all of the vicissitudes of life in this era of history. These gods are too numerous to count, and many are thought to be very near, perhaps in the location in which people are living.

One discovers by reading the ancient literature called the *Vedas*, a Sanskrit word meaning wisdom, that this wisdom provides guidance on how to understand the role of these gods, how to worship them, and how to find healing and guidance in reference to them. A few of these ancient people, often priests, were literate and able to consult the ancient literature that was present, consisting of three collections of writings: the Upanishads,

---

by Klause K. Klostermaier, in which he carefully describes the several influences that shaped the rise of Hinduism and the resulting several branches of modern Hinduism (1–16).

6. Ferguson, *Exploring the Spirituality of the World Religions*, 85.

Bhagavad Gita, and the Dhammapada.[7] It was the Upanishads that gave the most guidance about the Divine and ways of understanding life, although the other two pieces of literature were illustrative and anecdotal, providing the readers with examples of life's complexities and how to deal with them.

Two of the gods present in the belief system and described in the literature, Indra and Varuna, stand out in that they were believed to have power over human and social activities, not just events in the natural world. Human beings were seen as having an inner essence, called *atman*, that is the source of contact with the Divine and helps those on the spiritual journey to navigate through the worrisome insecurities and anxieties of human life as they seek wisdom and guidance. The navigation included the concept of overcoming the negative consequences of *karma-samsara*, the cosmic and personal laws of cause and effect by which one's thoughts and deeds determine what happens in this life and in lives to come. The gods have the power to help in this challenge with its range of threats to human welfare, and may ultimately guide one to *moksha* or spiritual liberation.[8]

Another accent in classical Hinduism stressed guidelines for right living and orderly social structures. These guidelines were in some measure a response to the changes brought about by the arrival of the Aryan population. For example, these new immigrants led the way in clearing large sections of land in order to make it available for agriculture. The people became dependent upon the fields for their livelihood. In addition, kings replaced local chieftains who had ruled over small regions, and these kings developed cities and regional kingdoms. Social classes emerged and formed the outline of new guidelines for behavior and the structures of a new social order. A guiding set of rules based on age and gender developed, called the *Sutras*, that confirmed these structures. In addition, there was a more developmental understanding of the stages of life: the student stage, the household stage, the retirement stage, and, following directly from retirement, the ascetic and contemplative stage in the last years of one's life.[9] The four-caste system emerged, with the Brahmin class, the warrior class, the commerce class, and the handicraft class. The serfs or outcastes were numerous and served the four castes in many ways. This arrangement gave

---

7. See the excellent translation of one of these bodies of literature by Eknath Easwaran, *Upanishads*. In order to use of these resources, there was a measure of literacy in a small segment of the population.

8. This liberation was understood to be freedom from the confines of the karma cycle and reincarnation.

9. As one reads the life of Gandhi, one sees these stages of life illustrated.

society more structured patterns of life and patterns of behavior (*dharma*) that were expected, although the society remained fundamentally unjust with the presence of the outcastes.

As people settled into these accents and patterns, there was the inevitable set of questions about whether they were just and how one might understand the best way to manage life. The people sought knowledge to guide them, less the kind of knowledge about how to function in order to carry out one's responsibilities and more about understanding existence and how to overcome the bondage that was a given ingredient in daily life. Often a priest consulted the ancient literature (the *Upanishads*) and guided the people from these writings. This literature suggested personal transformation through mystical knowledge rather than direct challenge to the unjust social structure. One could find a fulfilling (spiritual) pathway by turning inward through meditation and contemplation. As one turned inward, one could become enlightened, discover insight, and gain understanding that would lead to serenity and ultimately to *moksha* (spiritual liberation). One could encounter *Brahman*, the inherent power of all that exists and the power that controls the world. Brahman is the source of all that exists and the power that holds everything together, a Hindu belief that the divine essence is inherent in all that exists. Brahman is not a personal God, but the energy that animates all of reality and shapes it purpose and order.[10] Regional and family gods were thought by many to be manifestations of Brahman.

This contact with Brahman guides the individual and groups in the their personal and social behavior. There is a pattern of life that is ethical in character, including non-injury, truthfulness, chastity, freedom from greed, and a range of mental and spiritual virtues and practices. Our point in this brief summary is that these beliefs and practices are the result of practicing the way of mystical *devotion*, a pattern of life in which one finds one's way through opening inward by practicing meditation and contemplation. This prevailing point of view and practice became less about looking to the natural world for guidance and spiritual direction and more about the inward search through mystical practices, discovering the Divine that is within you and following its ways. As one seeks this mystical way, wisdom and knowledge are revealed and give guidance to individual behavior and ultimately may lead to more just social structures.

10. Ferguson, *Exploring the Spirituality of the World Religions*, 89–99.

Section One: Ways of Understanding Transcendence in the Premodern World

PREMODERN BUDDHISM

The origins and early development of Buddhism are easier to trace in that this religion had a specific founder, who was called Buddha. He attracted many followers due to his insightful teaching, extraordinary leadership, and the model of his life. Buddhism was a somewhat later development than Hinduism, coming to life in India in the fifth century BCE and developing in the fourth century BCE. It too was a religion and way of life that did not ignore looking outward to nature for guidance, but primarily sought freedom from suffering by turning inward.

Siddhartha Gautama (sometimes spelled Gotama) was born in approximately 563 BCE in Northeast India. The context in which he was born had the beginnings of Hinduism with its many gods and the suggested patterns of life found in the Vedas. The class structure existed, and there were cultic practices and the pattern of the ethical life described in the code of duties or *dharmas*. The Brahmin, the privileged and ruling class, was an integral part of the social structure, enjoyed many of its benefits, and provided spiritual guidance. In Siddhartha's location and to some extant across India, their spiritual leadership was being questioned, given their privileged status. Small groups had begun to form that were calling for social change and teaching the sacredness of life, nonviolence, the limitations of some of the cultic practices, and a more just social order.

Siddhartha grew up in in a wealthy family with a long tribal lineage and was provided with every luxury. The young prince was handsome, gifted, and had both the capabilities and promise of becoming a regional king or tribal leader following the death of his father. He was married with a child, and his pathway into the future looked attractive and secure. In his twenties, he began to feel somewhat discontent with his way of life, briefly left the compound, and observed the suffering of the common people. Tradition describes what are called the *Four Passing Sights*: an old and decrepit man representing old age, a person racked with disease, a corpse, and a monk with a shaved head who had withdrawn from the world. He was moved by these sights that spoke of the harsh realities of life and the ever-present psychic suffering of humankind. He achieved an "awakening," left his privileged surroundings (including his wife and child), and devoted the next six years to solitude, fasting, and poverty, called the *Great Renunciation*.

During these years of dedication and an ascetic and sacrificial lifestyle, seeking the bliss of oneness with ultimate reality, he became disillusioned and turned to private meditation. The Buddhist tradition teaches that he sat under a tree known as Bo (Bodhi or enlightenment) and ultimately achieved and experienced *nirvana*. He then began to teach others a middle way, one that rejects the extremes of asceticism and privileged wealth and luxury, and emphasizes the way of enlightenment. Soon, he attracted many others around him in this new calling to a spiritual way. His teaching was not primarily speculative, but based on the transformation of consciousness and virtues that might be summarized in the following four categories.[11]

1. *Metta*: lovingkindness
2. *Kauna*: compassion
3. *Mudita*: gentleness
4. *Upekkha*: equanimity

The movement began to grow, and in time expanded beyond the boundaries of India into East Asia. Early on, there were some differences among the spiritual leaders of the new Buddhist religion, and it gradually separated into various groups in new locations with slightly different patterns of belief and practice. It is an interesting story of religious development, reflecting new cultures and ways of life.[12] But it is beyond our purpose to attempt to trace this pattern of growth in detail at this point; our objective is rather to underline the primary religious outlook common to nearly all of these expressions of Buddhism.

Its four foundational observations about the nature of human life are well known and may be summarized in the following way:

1. Life is filled with suffering (*dukka*), and human sorrow is nearly universal. This observation about suffering carries with it the meaning that our lives are generally not what we would like them to be. Buddhist teachers point out that none of us will escape old age and we will all be forced to deal with pain and disease. The insight about suffering carries with it the observation that we suffer not just physically, but emotionally as well. Buddhists have acknowledged these harsh realities.
2. Buddhist teaching goes on to affirm that the cause of human suffering is attachment and craving (*tanha*). We have an insatiable desire to have and possess a wide range of things: objects of beauty, wealth,

---

11. Ferguson, *Spiritual Pathway*, 104.
12. All of the great religions of the human family have had patterns of growth that have evolved and changed from their initial beginnings.

property, reputation, power, and control in relationships. We soon find out that once we receive what we desire, what we have still does not meet our expectations and we have placed unrealistic expectations on the objects of our desire. We find ourselves in a vicious cycle, the cycle of *karma-samsara*, and we long for relief.

3. Buddhists affirm that there can be an end to suffering. We must let go of our craving and root out our need for attachments and possessions. In order to do so, we need a fundamental change of attitude; we must learn to accept the realities of life and acknowledge our current situation. We do so by making a fundamental shift in our lives. We begin by sharing our wealth and possessions with others, and as our attitude shifts from "I" to "we," we abandon our craving and we are able to find relief from the consequences of our selfish actions. We begin to experience joy and inner peace.

4. The fourth noble truth is to move toward transformation and spiritual liberation. We turn to a different route of life and begin to follow the Eightfold Path.

This path is made up of attitudes and actions:[13]

1. The first, as one might guess, is that we must maintain the right view, to keep focus on the goal of seeking spiritual liberation and enlightenment. Not infrequently, we take our eye off the ball and fumble life's opportunities for joy and inner peace. We need to acknowledge that life is transient and painful, to cultivate an enlightened awareness of the realities of life, and to gain self-knowledge. We must have the courage to see.

2. The second is that we must have the right intention about our goals and the resulting attitudes and actions. We need to free ourselves from both ignorance and delusion; life is not about craving and accumulating possessions. It is about fully realizing that the essence of life is lovingkindness, empathy, and compassion.

3. We then begin to change and improve the ways we communicate. We practice right speech filled with wisdom and the full acceptance and affirmation of others. We speak in loving ways that are filled with respect

---

13. See the book by Lama Surya Das *Awakening the Buddha Within* for a very good treatment of the EightFold Path.

and trust.[14] We avoid falsehoods and using language to hurt others, and we find the right ways to communicate the truth that is filled with beauty and wisdom. We love others by the way we communicate.

4. With the right view and right intention, we can proceed to the right action. We can begin to practice the art of finding positive and constructive ways to help others and be kind and benevolent. This also means that we avoid harmful actions such as causing others to suffer by our selfishness and insensitivity. And of course we do not steal from others.

5. To accomplish these goals, we become aware that we need to find the right livelihood. A great deal of time is spent in our work; it has an enormous influence on our lives and shapes our attitudes and behavior. The way we make a living is fundamental to our well-being and influences us in a wide variety of ways. It will both influence and reflect our deepest commitments and values. We learn how to love the people in our world through our work and we must avoid a pattern of work that harms people.

6. It requires, then, that we make the right effort to develop practices that nurture our spiritual lives and lead us in the pathway toward maturity, empathy, and compassion. We must cultivate those skills that will enable and empower us to make a positive contribution to individual lives and a just social order.

7. In order to achieve these goals, we must cultivate the right attitude and spirit. It is to practice right mindfulness, paying close attention to the present moment and staying in touch with what is happening around us and what is going on inside of us. We must become authentic human beings, full of integrity, and living in a truthful way.

8. And, as we set these goals of life, we need to have the right concentration. We must stay focused and committed to these goals and practices, and not be led astray by the values of a selfish and materialistic culture.

To stay on course and integrate the values of the eight elements of this spiritual pathway, we will need, as the Buddha and his early followers taught, to engage in a several practices that get us in spiritual shape. Buddhist teaching has a wide variety of practices that help us achieve the goals of Buddhist way. Buddha and his followers were fond of lists describing ways to get and stay on the pathway that leads to spiritual liberation. For

---

14. See the small book by Thich Nhat Hanh *How to Love*, 22.

example, there are two Truths, three Dharma Seals, three Doors of Liberation, three Jewels, four Immeasurable Minds, five Powers, seven factors of Awakening, twelve Links of Interdependent Co-Arising, and several other patterns of growth toward spiritual liberation and enabling the Buddha spirit to emerge in one's life. Lama Surya Das, a contemporary Buddhist teacher, lists the following qualities of life that characterize the mature practitioner of Buddhism:[15]

- appreciating the present moment,
- knowing one's distinctiveness,
- caring about friendships,
- finding calm and serenity,
- feeling inner harmony,
- being more efficient with daily tasks,
- and expressing compassion toward others and sensing a clear purpose in life.

We turn now to another directional metaphor and family of religions, the Abraham monotheistic religions of Judaism, Christianity, and Islam, each of which teaches that we must *reach upward* to discern the revelation of God and live in faithful obedience to God.

---

15. Das, *Awakening the Buddha Within*, 97–129.

4

Reaching Upward
The Ways of Faithfulness and Obedience

As I look back across the years of my life and give close attention to my spiritual development, I realize how profoundly I have been influenced and nurtured by the two ways I have described as a means of building a thoughtful way of discerning transcendence and, in many cases, establishing a faithful relationship with God or Transcendence. I have referenced the pattern of discovering in nature the evidence of God's creation and presence; and I have noted that by looking outward and opening inward with reflection and self-awareness I found a spiritual home with the One whose presence I have felt. I have sensed that Transcendence is personal and relational. Initially, I *extended outward*, especially in the earlier years of spiritual formation, to learn more about Transcendence, about God, creator and sustainer of all that exists. Had I lived in the premodern era, without the benefit of learning from great prophets and a scientific understanding of the natural world, I would have still been humbled before nature's power and beauty. I would have honored the creator, limited in depth as my spiritual capacity may have been. I then *turned inward* and felt the touch of the divine hand. I felt the mysterious presence of being created in the image of God and wondered where my mind and consciousness, the feelings of love, and the need for wholeness came from. I said with Rumi, "Our aching

Section One: Ways of Understanding Transcendence in the Premodern World

for God is His guarantee,"[1] and sought to make contact with the Divine through a range of intellectual inquiries and devotional practices.

Out of these experiences and the commitments that followed from them, I have oriented my life to their presence and remained mindful about the intimations of God's loving presence in my life. Later, with a greater measure of understanding and a deeper and more profound range of experience, I wrote a book entitled *Mindful Spirituality*, a series of daily reflections that invited readers to use the book of readings as a helpful way of relating to the Divine. I divided the book into three sections, one on seeing the presence of God in nature, one on sensing the presence of God within, and a third on *reaching upward* to God to understand what appeared to be *revelation* and then living faithfully in reference to this revelation as it expressed in some measure God's will. This third quest to understand what is believed to be revelation from God became central in my spiritual journey.

With a questioning mind and a longing heart, I followed this third way and reached upward as a way to understand and practice ways of connecting with the God. The way I went about this endeavor was to take full advantage of the wisdom of great teachers and prophets, the model of their lives, and the persuasiveness of their teaching. I sensed that they were attempting to understand divine revelation. They often taught that God has come to us in a variety of ways, and especially in Jesus, and that his life and teaching became revelatory. I also became involved in the church and some of its subgroups designed for students and received guidance and nurture. These experiences invited me to *reach upward* to God in a faith-based relationship, to learn and practice what is thought to be divine guidance, and to follow it faithfully. I responded in a positive way to this invitation and have followed this pathway across the years, gaining a more mature understanding of both the guiding narrative and the spiritual pathway.

I have looked back on these early years and reflected on the ways I was influenced and guided. I began in this reflection with the observation that what has come before us shapes our understanding of life, the settings in which we live, and the spiritual pathways we follow (or reject). I noted that this observation is even more profoundly true for those who lived in the premodern world. They were given a narrative and a pathway to follow, often without a lot of choice. In many ways, they were products of the way their narrative had developed over time. In a very real sense we are as well, although we may have more self-awareness and choice given

---

1. Mafi, *Rumi Day by Day*, 159.

our knowledge of how to manage and benefit from exposure to centuries of learning. We may be more self-aware, better informed, and better able to make wise decisions about our future, yet as we look at the condition of our world, we wonder if our advanced understanding and knowledge have led us to a better and safer place. So we underline that even our decisions based on insight and understanding will be filled with and shaped by our past experience and the context in which we have lived. Had I grown up in Pakistan, I may have become a Muslim or in India a Hindu. We inherit a mindset and worldview from our surroundings. In my adult years, I have reached upward with devotion, but also with disciplined inquiry and critical awareness of the way the Christian narrative has developed.

One of the ways we moderns have used our history and past experience is to find a thread of meaning in what may appear on the surface to be a somewhat random pattern of events. We have said that in this quest we hope to and may find the presence of some form of transcendence or Transcendence that provides it all with meaning, giving creation, the flow of history, and the pattern of our lives some order and purpose. We often use religious categories as well as those of the social and natural sciences to describe this transcendence. It has been a primary way to understand our past and provide categories of understanding for our present challenges and guidance for the future. Often, it is through religious beliefs and practices that the human family has sought to understand the world and, from past experience how to live wisely and well within it. "I was led by God" and "God's will be done on earth as it is in heaven" are common phrases in religious settings.

In many cases, we may have forgotten many of the details of our past experience, but they too have shaped our outlook and values almost more than we know. We inherit religious beliefs and values from what we have experienced and been taught. Our past and the context in which we live inform our struggle to find a source of wisdom, guiding values, and life's meaning. From this base, humans have asked whether there are transcendent principles or a personal Transcendence that will guide and empower them to live safely and constructively into the future.

We answer "yes" and add history and religious belief (what we consider to be revelatory) to our way of understanding our lives. We have already described how the human family has looked outward to nature for clues that suggest healthy and life-giving patterns of life. Does nature suggest a good way to live? Perhaps there are principles of order, structure,

Section One: Ways of Understanding Transcendence in the Premodern World

and development in nature that suggest healthy patterns of life; it is nature that sustains us with food and the sun that warms. In addition to looking outward to the natural world for guidance and needed resources for living, humans have also looked inward, using their minds and emotions to discern patterns of wisdom and guidance for life. We have turned to prayer, meditation, and other devotional practices, sensing in them the presence of Transcendence and a whisper of guidance.

I want now to describe a third spiritual direction or pathway, that of reaching upward, one that has much in common with those that we have already described, but has some different emphases. It is the spiritual way of the Abrahamic monotheistic religions, which has guided so many in their quest for an understanding of Transcendence and direction in life. It guides seekers and pilgrims to look upward (a third directional metaphor) to encounter Transcendence and understand what is believed to be divine revelation that teaches a way into the future and how to manage threats, find meaning, and improve life. Many of the great teachers of wisdom in this tradition, both women and men, claimed to have received divine guidance and empowerment from their encounter with Transcendence, and from this encounter they have offered their followers ways of understanding the spiritual life. There are several expressions religious ideas and patterns in this family of religions, but I want to focus on the main three Abrahamic monotheistic religions of Judaism, Christianity, and Islam, and note the ways that their primary founders, Moses, Jesus, and Muhammad guided their followers.[2] Essentially what to believe and how to act were claimed to come from "on high," i.e., it was divine revelation, and the followers were expected to reach upward *in faith* to connect with the Divine and to live faithfully and obediently in reference to what they learned.

I want to say a brief word about what we mean by "faith," in that it might suggest that the decision to endorse this course of action in faith means that it is uninformed and may lead to a naïve, distorted, and possibly harmful way of life. This occasionally does happen, and in many cases the pathway becomes narrow, exclusive, tribal, and cultic in character. However, the word *faith* does not mean blind and uninformed; it means that we believe there is a God who is the very ground of being, truly Other. God is a different form of reality, far above and beyond our capacity to capture the full meaning, given the limitations of intelligence and language, traditional and

---

2. Women surrounded these great religious leaders and helped them to shape the guiding narrative they left to the human family.

cultural patterns, and categories of understanding. The best of our patterns of explanation may contain helpful pointers, signs, and symbols that point to Transcendence. Yet our descriptions remain metaphorical in character.

As we use the word *faith*, we need to be sure of its meaning. Our understanding must have at least three dimensions if it is to fully encase its true character.

1. As we place our faith in a religious narrative, we need to be sure that this narrative is as truthful to reality as we can possibly get. It must have credibility, integrity, logical order, and historical accuracy. As far as possible, it must be partially evidence based, although the leap of faith will still need to be taken. It must correspond to what we know is truthful. Faith is not "believing what everybody else knows ain't so." Yes, as Søren Kierkegaard maintained, faith takes us beyond the realm of scholarly accuracy, the laws of logic, and simple common sense, but not to the point of endorsing superstition and the historical accuracy of legends.

2. Secondly, faith is the establishment of a relationship; it is to place our trust in the Transcendence or God in a personal way, one that engages the right side of brain and calls forth love and dedication, not exclusively scientific or mathematical proof. We place our faith in a personal Transcendence who loves, forgives, empowers, and guides us in a way that enables us to thrive and flourish. Our faith empowers us to become healthy and mature people. It is the spark that inflames our soul and lights the way of the soul's journey to a good life and eternal bliss.

3. And third, faith calls forth acting on what we have endorsed. It is commitment that engages us and calls on us to use spiritual practices to cultivate a spiritual way of life and to act on the principles of love and compassion. As James, the author of an epistle in the New Testament, reminds us: "faith without deeds is dead" (Jas 2:26). We must get involved for it all to work well.

This third way to *reach upward* and embrace Transcendence, then, is to place our faith in a personal God, a trustworthy narrative that is revelatory, and follow a spiritual pathway that is nurturing and life giving.

Section One: Ways of Understanding Transcendence in the Premodern World

PREMODERN JUDAISM

I begin with a brief sketch of the formation of the religion of the Hebrew people because it provided a foundational history, information, and insight not just to its own adherents, but also to both Christianity and to Islam. We first learn about the Hebrew people by tracing their family tree back to a nomadic tribe that lived on the Arabian Peninsula. The life of these ancestors was tribal in character and they lived on the edge of the surrounding desert. Their culture was similar to the other tribes of this period of history. Like other Stone Age tribes, they wandered across the region in search of food and to find pasture for their animals. They were likely polytheistic in their beliefs and had a range of divinities that reflected their many needs, feelings, and fears. In time, they began to move northward into Mesopotamia in search of a setting that provided more resources.

The story for all three of the great religious traditions begins with a description of Abraham, who traveled north and settled in Ur of the Chaldeans, a settlement on the Euphrates River. The biblical story of Abraham, living likely about 2000 BCE[3] (Gen 17:1–8 and 22:15–18), describes him as one who believed in a single God, and that he was called by God to travel west to another region bordering the Mediterranean Sea, called Canaan. He gathered his family and collected his possessions and set out, "going without knowing." It was a bold action of faith. This story became central to Judaism, and in time to Christianity and Islam. Abraham became a model of faith and faithfulness for all three great religions, although each one interprets the story a bit differently. For Judaism, the story is an essential part of the foundation of their narrative and describes Abraham as being a true believer in *Yahweh* (God), who faithfully led the people to a "promised land" and gave them guidance on how to live and have hope for their future.

The story of Abraham's travels and his arrival is full of intrigue, drama, and many lessons for life. Yet what holds all of these details together is Abraham's faith in Yahweh, the one and only God, and his effort to live faithfully in reference to his beliefs. Following the life of Abraham, the story continues with many dramatic events and foundational lessons for the Hebrew people. The next high point in the development of Judaism is the story of Moses (late 1500s BCE to middle 1400s BCE).[4]

---

3. Some scholars date the life of Abraham at a different time, perhaps the 1800s BCE, challenging the more traditional dating. One commonly used date is that he lived within the years 1996–1821 BCE.

4. Again, there is some discussion among scholars about precise dates.

Reaching Upward

The story of Moses is well known and is told in the book of Exodus. He was born to a Hebrew woman, an immigrant slave in Egypt who was fearful that her baby would not survive if she kept him. She places him on a small raft on the banks of the Nile, hoping he will be found and given a safe and nurturing home. An Egyptian princess discovers the baby and brings him to her home, the royal palace. He grows up as prince in the household of the Pharaoh, and during that time he learns of his Hebrew heritage. As a young man, he sees an Egyptian soldier abusing a Hebrew worker, and he slays the soldier. Moses knows he must flee and spends time as a refugee in a setting north of Egypt. In time, as Moses engages in prayer and meditation, he hears the voice of God and is transformed. He senses that he is called by God to set the Hebrews free from their slavery in Egypt. He returns to Egypt and confronts Pharaoh, and when Pharaoh refuses to free the Hebrew people, plagues cause suffering to the Egyptian people. Moses then leads the Hebrew people across the Red Sea, and they travel a good distance into modern-day Jordan. Moses dies, but Joshua leads the people across the Jordon River into the "promised land" of Canaan (Palestine).

Out of this story and the earlier one of Abraham's life on the Euphrates River come the major tenets of premodern Judaism. Based on a dramatic and complex narrative, the following themes emerge as the heartbeat of premodern Judaism:[5]

1. The primary belief that holds the others together is that there is a transcendent God who is personal and engaged in human affairs. This God is called *Yahweh*,[6] and it is Yahweh who is the creator and sustainer of all that exists and engaged with all people and especially those who become the Hebrew people. For them, Yahweh is present, yet other or transcendent, not just a bigger and stronger human; although God is described in metaphorical and anthropological ways. God is generally understood and described with the language that describes human beings. Yet it is clear that God is above and beyond human frailties, although personal, so that it is possible for humans to be in relationship with Transcendence.

2. It was Yahweh who created all there is with intention and meaning. It follows that the creation came into being for a purpose; it was more

---

5. Once again, I draw upon the biblical story and some of my previous writing in the book *Exploring the Spirituality of the World Religions*, 153–54.

6. Other names for God or the gods existed in the languages of the era, and at least one other (*Elohim*) is present in the biblical story.

Section One: Ways of Understanding Transcendence in the Premodern World

than just a big bang, although this may have been God's way of creating. The vast universe is not just random change and development, a cosmic accident, but called good and believed to have inherent value and purpose and therefore ought to be respected and sustained. It is there for humans to use, and in this use, because it is gift from God, it is to be sustained in wise ways and honored as a divine gift. Humans are to be good stewards of the creation.

3. Implied in this way of understanding creation, which includes the origin of the human family, is that humans are created in the image of God, have responsibilities, are given ethical guidelines (e.g., the Ten Commandments), and have the capacity to create a just social order. Responsibility, based on compassion and justice, is underlined. Over the years, patterns of social and personal behavior were codified and became law, often thought to be sacred law or *Torah*, as contained in the first five books of the Hebrew Bible.

4. This belief in Yahweh provided a way for these early Hebrew people (Jewish people) to understand their history. They felt chosen and responsible to join with Yahweh in the ongoing processes of the creation, or to say it another way, they believed they had a special history to reveal the purpose of God and to follow the will and way of God in their individual and common life. As they were called to particular way of life, one based upon the philanthropic principles of love and justice, they attempted to create a social code with guidance on how to manage their corporate life. It is Torah or Law that guided them. Priests and rulers built their social order around a range of living patterns, many that are religious in character, which have come down to us in the Pentateuch and other writings (the Law and the Prophets).

5. Gradually, over time, these people become a nation, led by kings whose names and stories have influenced the flow of human history. The accounts of David and Solomon are familiar to all of us. Great prophets such as Isaiah and Jeremiah, with their extraordinary teaching, called for justice and peace. These prophets interpreted a central event in their lives, the Babylonian captivity, as a serious setback and an opportunity to live more faithfully and cultivate a vision for a new pattern of life, one that was faithful to Yahweh and spoke to their current patterns of injustice. The Psalms provide worship and devotional resources and the wisdom literature, e.g., Proverbs, gives practical

guidance on how to live wisely and well. Holidays in the Jewish calendar call to mind the significant historical events and ways God has guided this remarkable minority of people.

Out of these biblical stories and the influence of the Hebrew people has come another narrative, the story of a Jewish man whose life and teachings became the core of modern Christianity.

PREMODERN CHRISTIANITY

The formation and development of Christianity is also complex, not unlike the early formation of Judaism. Reputable scholars, teachers, priests, and pastors have spent lifetimes studying these early beginnings that led to fully developed religions.

As one of these interpreters, I know the risks of distortion that exist in summaries, the importance of sound historical methods, and the need to use thoughtful and wise hermeneutical principles. So with a base of knowledge upon which to draw, I would like to mention some foundational components of early Christianity.

1. It is important to stress initially that the Christian religion did have its origins in the context, events, social patterns, and beliefs of premodern Judaism. We start with the observation that Jesus was a Jew, although perhaps a marginal one, coming as he did from the Galilee in the north rather than in the center of Judaism in Jerusalem. He was born into a family that participated in Jewish practices and attended a synagogue either in Nazareth or a neighboring village. His birth is described as being in Bethlehem (a village near Jerusalem), surrounded by Jewish practices, and as the fulfillment of prophetic teaching.[7] His parents had traveled there to participate in a Roman census and perhaps to participate in Jewish holiday celebrations. Some Jewish people identified him as the expected *Messiah* or *Christ*, and the story describes astrologers from the Middle East who came to pay homage to a new king. His was a practicing Jew in his early life in Galilee, and as he began his public ministry it was carried out largely in a Jewish frame of reference, although largely in Galilee, where there was a more diverse population. He often taught and healed in synagogues, and his teaching drew heavily on the Hebrew Bible. There were many who

7. Some scholars have suggested that Jesus was actually born in Nazareth.

Section One: Ways of Understanding Transcendence in the Premodern World

marveled at his teaching and others who resisted his teaching. He was indeed a creative interpreter of the Hebrew Bible, inviting readers to understand its message in new and life-changing ways.

2. One of his primary followers and interpreters of his life and death was a well-educated Jew, a dedicated Pharisee, known to us as the apostle Paul. Paul was careful to place the life, death, and his belief in the resurrection of Jesus within a Jewish frame of reference, describing him as the long-expected Messiah. But Paul went beyond Jewish hopes and expectations and identified Jesus as Savior and Lord, the full expression of God's presence and the source of eternal life for all people. He faced opposition from Jewish leaders and priests because he called Jesus divine and because he understood the life and teaching of Jesus as having universal meaning, available for all people, rather than having a more narrow sectarian and tribal tone. Yet in this bold interpretation, Paul remained within a Jewish frame of reference.[8]

3. In time, the new orientation based on the Jesus event was questioned within the structures of Judaism as it took the form of a new religion for all people. The ministry and writings of Paul were foundational for this new religious orientation, and he generally spoke of this new orientation as an extension Judaism. But many of the Jewish leaders in Jerusalem did see it as a dangerous heresy. It lost some of its Jewish overtones as it spread outside of the Jewish centers and was endorsed by Gentiles. As it was proclaimed and viewed more positively, many churches began to appear across the expanse of the Roman Empire. As the belief system developed in succeeding generations, the majority of Christians saw Jesus and the new religion as a God-guided and true outgrowth of Judaism.

4. A great deal of attention was given in the attempt to clarify the identity of Jesus, the content of his teaching, and the meaning of his death with the accompanying belief in his resurrection. As scholars and faithful followers struggled in this endeavor, they drew upon an oral tradition, the emergence of written documents (the letters of Paul, other writings, and finally the four biblical Gospels), and the mindset of the time in which they believed. They did come to believe that Jesus was divine, and that in a variety of ways through his teaching and the events of his death and resurrection, Jesus became Lord and Savior and the focal

8. See Romans 9–11.

point of new religion. They underlined the primary teaching of Jesus to be the kingdom of God or *the power and presence of God* that has come and is available for all people, healing them, guiding them, and giving them the assurance of God's eternal and everlasting love. God was no longer primarily located in a temple in Jerusalem, but present to all people, who are invited to claim by faith God's reigning presence and healing love. They are invited to become a part of a community called *the church* to extend the message of God's love and, as followers of Jesus, to serve as he did in the ministries of compassion and a commitment to justice.

5. I find myself living now with this understanding of those early centuries of belief, although reworking much of what they taught and sought to explain. In time, it became the New Testament. I identify with them in my honest searching. Yet, with this deep empathy, I am also keenly aware that they were children of their time. With the new understanding given to us by the rise of science, historical-critical scholarship, global challenges, changing worldviews, and a dozen other factors, I remain in the Christian family but with a view more in keeping with a contemporary way of viewing the world.[9] I remain in the family largely because it seems to me that Jesus got it right as he fulfilled his roles as prophet, teacher, and healer. He gave himself to finding and living by the truth, teaching and living the centrality of love and compassion, and prophetically challenging all forms of unjust governance and practice.

PREMODERN ISLAM

Another religion rooted in the Abrahamic tradition, Islam, came to life in the early seventh century of the Common Era on the Arabian Peninsula. It too is global in character, and as with its cousins, Judaism and Christianity, there are Muslim communities in all parts of the world. In the past several decades, the importance of Islam has been recognized in part because a small minority of Muslims have used violent means to advance their cause, but also, and more importantly, its finest leaders have guided Muslims to be

---

9. On occasion, this view and related views have been called progressive or neoliberal.

Section One: Ways of Understanding Transcendence in the Premodern World

responsible citizens of the world, to invite understanding across religious boundaries, and to seek a more just and humane world.

The religion has its beginnings in Mecca on the Arabian Peninsula, a region that had well-developed trade practices, and its citizens were therefore exposed to other cultures and new ideas. There was the limited presence of the beliefs of Judaism and Christianity in the region. It was in this setting that Muhammad, the great prophet of Islam, was born in 570 CE. After losing his parents at an early age, his paternal uncle stepped in and wisely guided him. As he matured, he became active in the business and cultural life of the region. He married an older woman, a widow, who provided a stable environment, yet he remained troubled in his young adulthood. He did not find the religious context of his clan and tribe very attractive and began to speak out boldly about reform. He withdrew from society, engaged in meditation in a nearby cave on Mount Hira, and began to have revelations that he understood as coming directly from God or *Allah*. Though not fully literate, he recited these revelations, and friends and followers then carefully write them down. Many of them were later to become the essential content of the Quran.

In 622 CE, he began his work as the prophet of a new religion. Not without some resistance and difficulty, the new religious orientation became a community of believers, which embodied a comprehensive religious worldview, one guided by the Quran. There are five foundational beliefs or pillars that gave Islam its foundation:

1. The first is the belief in the unity and oneness of God, a shared belief with Judaism and Christianity and attributed to Abraham.
2. The second is that God (Allah) makes the divine will known to humans through messengers or prophets.
3. The third is the affirmation that God is the creator of all there is. God created the universe and gave it order and purpose.
4. A fourth foundational belief is that the sovereign God (Allah) will make a final judgment on whether people have followed the divine will and way.
5. The fifth pillar of belief is that there will be a community of faith (*Ummah*) that will worship Allah and guide believers in faith and obedience.

As with most religious traditions, there are practices in Islam that are the outgrowth of the foundational belief system. There are primarily five practices, although in time a full pattern of behavior for nearly every aspect of life became prescribed. These five pillars of practice are:

1. The first, called the *Shahadah*, is to confess that there is no god but Allah and that Muhammad is Allah's messenger.
2. The second (*Salat*) is that a true believer should pray five times per day facing the *Ka'bah*, the sacred cubicle in Mecca.
3. The third fundamental practice is the annual expectation of almsgiving by all believers, primarily to help those in need.
4. The fourth pillar of the list of five practices is Ramadan, the month of fasting.
5. The fifth practice for all who are able is the *Hajj*, the pilgrimage to Mecca to honor the founder and founding of Islam.

There are times when a true believer may be called on to carry out a *jihad*, a profound effort or struggle to sustain the straight path of Islam. The practice, at times inaccurately interpreted as a violent act against an enemy, should not be seen primarily as an act of violence or warfare, but a concerted effort to advance and spread Islam. Unfortunately, it has occasionally been understood as permitting an overly aggressive way to achieve the goals of Islam.

Muhammad himself, in the early days of Islam, was active in its spread, and across the centuries, much like that of Christianity, its followers have carried this religion to many parts of the world. At times this widespread growth has caused some suffering to non-Muslims, but overall the effort has had a philanthropic purpose, to enable people to follow what Muslims believe is the straight path to follow Allah, or the one true God. In addition, as with Judaism and Christianity, the followers of Islam had differences, some of which could not be resolved, and Islam divided into separate units.

We turn now to exploring how these several religious orientations found their way into the modern world and how their religious beliefs and practices developed over this historical period.

Section Two

The Modern Quest to Understand and Connect with Transcendence

The way of the Bodhisattva was composed in India over twelve centuries ago, yet it remains remarkably relevant for our times. This classic text, written by the Indian sage, Shantideva, gives surprisingly up-to-date instructions for people like you and me to live sanely and openheartedly in a very troubled world.

—Pema Chödrön

5

Creation Spirituality
The Ways of Reason and Reflection

QUESTIONS ALONG THE WAY

WE ARE SHIFTING THE emphasis in this new section to the ways that we who live in the contemporary world seek to find traces of Transcendence (and transcendence), hoping to discern from these findings a spiritual way that will enable and empower us to manage our profound challenges and flourish. We are keenly aware, as we sift and sort intimations of transcendence, that reason, historical study, the social sciences, and scientific research will provide good explanations for most of these traces, hints, and whispers. The natural world, with all of its beauty, size, and power, can be described by science, although we are deeply awed as we gaze at our galaxy and reflect on the presence other galaxies. Might we be viewing the hand of the Creator? Where did all of this come from? How did being itself originate? Why is there something and not nothing? Others have looked at unusual and unique events in history and affirmed that they represent an act of God. Most of these occurrences have been given good historical explanations, but many people from certain faith traditions still maintain that they are divine interventions, truthful traces of Transcendence. The same questions surface as we observe and experience the profound human engagement of sensing the Divine as we pray and meditate. What do the moments of joy

Section Two: The Modern Quest to Understand and Connect with Transcendence

and peace tell us? There are good psychological explanations for these attempts to personally connect with Transcendence, yet those who engage in these practices sense that they are taken to a deeper level of equanimity and bliss than what occurs in a mere psychological experience. Even a deep and profound consciousness of the most spiritual person might be explained by brain research, yet there may be another dimension to this level of consciousness. And as we view the exemplary lives of such people as St. Francis, Mother Teresa, and Mahatma Gandhi, we ask if their testimony that they were led and empowered by God or Spirit is accurate. Might evolution and social conditioning, present in the religious traditions, sufficiently explain these lives, dedicated as they were to compassion, the relief of suffering, and the quest for justice? We ask whether the social and natural sciences fully explain the profound and universal truths and values they demonstrated. Were their views an "accident" of the evolutionary process? Or was there transcendent intentionality?

Part of our answer to these questions is to think in terms of both-and rather than either-or. The social and physical sciences continue to find convincing explanations for what exists and how it all works. I am persuaded that most of these scientific explanations for what has occurred in nature and in human history are valid, although continually refined. I am much less inclined, as I learn more, to use the God of the gaps argument to fill in what I don't understand. Those engaged in shaping modern religious thought, across most of the world's religions, have had to face the reality that we can no longer easily look at and describe what appear to be the unique and indescribable events in our history as the intervention of the Divine. For example, it may be hard to believe that God cut a swath through the *Red* Sea for Moses and the Hebrews as they escaped from Egypt. It may be that Moses and his followers crossed the *Reed* Sea in places where the ground was sufficiently firm to allow chariots with wheels to cross without sinking into wet sand. It was still a quite remarkable event, and in the mind of Moses, an event in which God was fully present. It also may be the case that Jesus really did heal the sick and demoniacs, and it was this belief that was in the minds and hearts of his faithful followers who saw the hand of God in this remarkable human being who healed people and gave them hope in difficult times. Yet the healing may have a psychological explanation as well. And it might be the case that Muhammad discovered great religious truths as he meditated on Mt. Hira, ones he believed came directly from Allah. But perhaps it is enough to say that these profound insights came from his meditation and concentration. We do know that they helped his contemporaries and followers deepen their faith and find guidance for life. Was it dictation from Allah or the profound sense of calling and spiritual truth of this dedicated person?

Some of the world's best minds have struggled with these questions about whether there is the presence of Transcendence in the natural world and human history. Some see Transcendence in these few remarkable happenings that we do not yet fully understand. There has been a wide range of answers, ones that I would like to summarize in three categories. The first and quite common answer among true believers is that there were miracles, especially in the founding events of the religions. There are slightly different definitions of *miracle*, but the way we are using the term is to describe an unusual, surprising, and often welcoming event that is not easily explained by natural or scientific laws. It is therefore thought to be the work of a divine or transcendent entry into the normal flow of events. It is an event that is improbable, an extraordinary occurrence that is thought to have a good consequence. Traditional *theism* has generally explained the extraordinary occurrences as the special entrance and action of God or a divine miracle.

A second view, called *pantheism*, maintains that the *Divine is reality or what happens in the universe*; the Divine is not transcendent in a separate place called *heaven*, but is the actual flow of events. The Divine is not above and beyond the events, but is fully present in the events. What happens in the universe is the manifestation of the becoming of God; what happens in the universe is an expression of the living God. This point of view, although with different language and practices, may in fact begin to cross over into a scientific view, especially as scientific answers are found to explain extraordinary events. If so, then do we really need to use religious language? Perhaps we do as we add concepts such as meaning and purpose.

A third view, one that has been present in embryonic form in earlier times, has resurfaced and provides a way of holding onto the view that there is a God who is transcendent. God is not just the actual events of the universe, but truly Transcendent and yet profoundly active in the natural world and the history of the universe. This is called *panentheism*, stressing that God doesn't just appear on certain occasions, providing a miraculous event that solves a problem and provides a way forward for particular people. God is fully present in (*pan-en theos*) the universe, in nature, and the flow of human history, yet separate and the very ground of being, the source and resource of all that exists. God is Other, yet interpenetrates the universe and is engaged with it. God is beyond space and time, yet is available as a source of creation and active in change and development, healing, and guidance. To explain these rare occurrences and experiences in a scientific way does not rule out the divine presence in these occurrences. Indeed, scientific inquiry may be a way of discovering the divine way.

As I review these three options of explaining what appear to be extraordinary, indeed unique events, I tend to understand them primarily within my frame of reference. As I reflect upon them and discuss them, I will tend to describe patterns of belief within the Christian tradition, in part because it is my path of faith and it is the one I have studied extensively. I will tend to draw upon Christian thought and practice as a way of illustrating how humans have understood the traces of transcendence. I will also tend to illustrate the way this understanding has changed because the world has changed, and the human way of understanding and describing the traces of transcendence has had to change in response to changing worldviews. Again, illustrations will come more from Christian understanding than other faith traditions, at least in this chapter. We do tend to draw upon our culture, language, and time and place in history to describe what we consider to be traces of transcendence. I want us to look at and reflect on two modern approaches that see the traces of transcendence in human history and scientific inquiry and ask whether we can find the Divine through their understanding and practices.[1]

CREATION SPIRITUALITY

There is a relatively recent spiritual movement within the larger Christian family, although with ecumenical and interfaith dimensions, called *creation spirituality*. It has affirmed a deep belief that God continues to be active in the ongoing process of creation and the flow of human history. However, the emphasis of this movement known as creation spirituality is focused on the goodness of the creation rather than human sinfulness and the need for God's unique activity of redemption. The God of love invites us to come along side and join in the ongoing process of creation. In the case of Christian spirituality, the emphasis is less upon sending Jesus to die for our sins to appease a judgmental God and more upon yielding to and

---

1. I do draw upon my own religious tradition, in some measure because I am better informed about it, to illustrate how modern religious thought has explored the theme of transcendence. It is certainly true that other traditions have been active in doing so as well.

Creation Spirituality

claiming the power and presence of God to heal, make whole, and care for the good earth. Jesus died because of our sins rather than for our sins. We acknowledge our faults and limitations, but rejoice in our personhood and seek to link with God in the formation of a more just and humane world.

THE HISTORICAL ROOTS OF CREATION SPIRITUALITY

Creation spirituality has been informed and shaped by a wide range of philosophical and religious thought across the centuries. Creation spirituality is not altogether new and has resurfaced with new dimensions and expressions. Its roots are widespread and include the normative literature of the great religions such as the Bible, the Quran, and the Upanishads. The concepts of this foundational literature have been integrated and made contemporary as they intersect with deep human need, the psychology of human development, and a postmodern worldview. It is not an easy task to trace all that has gone into the mix, but a glance back to the foundational literature, especially in the Bible, may help us in grasping the central components of creation spirituality.

The roots of creation spirituality are present in the Bible and found expression in Judaism and the early formation of the Christian faith, although the components were not specifically identified with that label. Yet the themes are present within the creation story in Genesis: "So God created humankind in the divine image, in the image of God, the Transcendent One created them; male and female God created them. God blessed them . . . God saw everything that he made, and indeed, it was very good" (Gen 1:27, 31a). It is clear in this first account of creation in Genesis that what God created was good. It was an original blessing rather than an experiment gone wrong.[2] Even in the second account of creation in Genesis 2 and 3, while there are verses that speak about human failing, there really is not a precise description of a cosmic "fall." There is a clear indication in the mythical story that humans have failed and are becoming aware of the issues of right and wrong. Implied in this account is that human beings are part of a good creation, yet have the challenges that we all experience. As we read chapters 2 and 3 of Genesis, we are reminded that evil is real; it is an accurate and realistic assessment, in mythical and story form, of human existence. What has been called *the fall* is a category imposed onto

---

2. See the book by Matthew Fox *Original Blessing* for a full development of this point of view.

the literature and yet it is not clearly present in the Genesis account. What our ancestors called *the fall* may be another name for evolution; we are becoming and have a ways to go.

It was much later that Christian theologians, perhaps more so than Jewish theologians, began to talk about original sin and depravity. Augustine (354–430 CE) wrote brilliantly about the problem of human sin, and even illustrated it from his own life in a remarkable way in his *Confessions*. He certainly pointed to human sin and articulated the doctrine of a cosmic fall of humankind. With great insight, he wrote about the difficulty of staying within the will of God apart from God's transforming grace. He spoke directly about the transformation that occurs as one embraces God and is empowered by God's Spirit (the power and presence of God). It was much later when another noted theologian, Anselm (1033–1109 CE), developed a theory of atonement that underlined the sinfulness of humankind and the need for the atoning death of Christ to satisfy the righteousness of God and the demands of righteousness and justice. In both of these theologians, we see the early statements of the doctrine of original sin, and therefore the need for the redemption that comes from embracing the atoning death and resurrection of Jesus Christ.

In was during the Reformation that this doctrine of original sin became a central component of Christian theology, especially in the Reformed tradition. John Calvin (1510–564 CE) carefully expressed the doctrine of original sin and the need for substitutionary atonement, one that would satisfy God's standard of righteousness. He maintained that God graciously took the initiative in the redemption of humankind by sending Jesus Christ to atone for our sins. Humans are unable to live up to the norms of righteousness that are required in order to receive God's full acceptance and love. But "God so loved the world that he gave his only son, so that everyone who believes in him may not perish but have eternal life" (John 3:16). Since his time, the Christian church has struggled with and debated about the capacity of humans to measure up to God's expectations and the need for saving grace. The issues surrounding free will and predestination are key elements in the conversation. We continue to live with this debate in the life of the contemporary Christian church with a spectrum of beliefs, ranging from the capacity of humans to live ethically and be affirmed by God and the incapacity of humans to measure up to God's expectations and the need for substitutionary atonement, understood as Christ's death as the means to atone for human sin and the acceptance of Christ's sacrificial death as means of gaining acceptance by God.

Creation spirituality is related to this subject and has sided with those who see humans as having the capacity to grow and develop into mature and ethical human beings. In fact, in many cases, it is the example of Jesus that inspires them and the acceptance of God's life-changing love that grounds them in the growth toward a mature and a flourishing life filled with joy and peace. We were created in the image of God, and with God's empowering grace we can become whole.

Other strands of Christian thought have entered into this conversation about creation spirituality and helped to shape it as a clear spiritual pathway. For example, within the Christian church, there has been the longstanding concern to find a way to hold two major beliefs together and to integrate them: that of the initiative of God to offer unconditional love and that of human freedom to claim it. It is the classic problem of affirming predestination and human free will at the same time. The New Testament, of course, is quoted to defend both foundational beliefs, with some quoting the apostle Paul to stress God's sovereignty and others citing the Gospels and the example of the spiritual journey of Jesus in order to define their views. On the Roman Catholic side, drawing heavily on the thought of Thomas Aquinas, there has been a lean toward preserving human freedom. Humans do have the capacity to reach up to God and receive God's loving presence and engage in spiritual practices to cultivate a deep spiritual pathway. With the assistance of the church in providing its priestly care and sacramental practices, humans can and do participate in living the spiritual life in order to maintain good standing in the eyes of God. The same may be said for the Orthodox tradition, although with quite a different history, theological understanding, and spiritual guidance. On the Protestant side, drawing upon Martin Luther and John Calvin, the Protestant family placed a very strong emphasis on the sovereign initiative of God. Humans, though sinful, are chosen and, with a strong belief in the Christ event, are empowered by the Holy Spirit. They are able to live a truly spiritual life. Within the Free Church tradition, there was clear guidance for each individual to open their heart to the power and presence of God and to engage in spiritual practices that would sustain them. The movement of creation spirituality has drawn upon and in many cases reacted to these theological dimensions within the church community.

Section Two: The Modern Quest to Understand and Connect with Transcendence

Nearly all of these several themes can feed into the pathway of creation spirituality, but there is a clear movement away from the need to be saved from our sins by Christ's atoning death (redemption) and a strong affirmation of God's good creation and our capacity to receive God's gracious love and move toward health and wholeness.

THE COMPONENTS OF CREATION SPIRITUALITY

In his book *Original Blessing*, Matthew Fox provides a chart that demonstrates the differences between the fall/redemption paradigm and the creation spirituality (or original blessing) paradigm. I will illustrate from the chart, selecting a few of the contrasts from the fairly long list.[3]

Fall/Redemption	Creation Spirituality
Begins with sin	Begins with God's creative energy
Emphasizes original sin	Emphasizes original blessing
Faith as thinking assent (Augustine)	Faith as trust
Patriarchal	Feminist and gender balanced
Ascetic	Aesthetic
Mortification of the body	Discipline toward birthing
Control of passions	Ecstasy, *eros*, and celebration of passion
Virtue lies in the will	Virtue lies in the passions
Passion is a curse	Passion is a blessing
God as Father	God as Mother, Child and Father
Suffering is wages for sin	Suffering is birth pains; all beings suffer

3. See Hall, "Creation Spirituality," as well as the book *Original Blessing* by Matthew Fox.

Creation Spirituality

Fall/Redemption	Creation Spirituality
Death is wages for sin	Death is a natural event
Science is not the only source of understanding	Science teaches us about nature
Dualistic (either/or)	Dialectic (both/and)
Spirit in opposition to matter	Spirit and matter integrated
Suspicious of the body	Welcoming of the body
Humility is to question your value	Humility is to like oneself
Be in control	Letting go
Pessimistic	Hopeful
Personal salvation	Salvation and healing for all
Theistic	Panentheistic
My religion is the only way	Deep ecumenism
Eternal life comes after death	Eternal life is now
Guilt, shame, and redemption	Gratitude and praise
Faith is in the intellect	Faith is in the imagination

There are some risks in providing a partial list as a summary; the full list provides a bit more clarity in the contrasts, although the above list does give us a helpful example of the paradigm shift in the theology undergirding creation spirituality. As I review the subjects in the rows, I find that some of these contrasts may be viewed as illustrating a continuum of emphasis rather than a sharp contrast, as for example the contrast between pessimism and hopefulness. It would not be accurate to say that those who are described as pessimistic have no or only a little bit of hope. Hope for them comes when they acknowledge their deep need and turn to God for reassurance. They do not have less hope, but describe its reality in reference to human sin and the need for God's grace. In addition, the categories may need a bit more expansion, although Matthew Fox does explain the chart of opposites in *Original Blessing* and other writing. As I read this material, I do sense that in some cases the categories tend to be "leans" rather than absolute positions, and some of the either-or categories of the list may be thought of as both-ands. I do want to underline that Matthew Fox provides clear contrasts and inspires us to be thoughtful and wise in our belief systems, but I also learn from this movement about the risk of moving toward a new set of absolutes and stereotyping those with other points of view.

Another summary of this new direction in finding a spiritual pathway is provided in the Rev. Dr. Sid Hall's "Creation Spirituality: The Six Essentials."[4] I will list his six essentials and offer some comment on each of them.

1. "The Universe, and all life within it, is fundamentally a blessing."

    I affirm that we need to make a shift in our outlook if we are inclined to be overly negative in assessing our condition as a human family, the welfare of planet earth, and indeed the whole universe. If we begin with a more positive outlook, we will likely have the motivation, insight, and energy to do our part in creating a healthier earth and a more just and humane world. There is so much that in is good and beautiful about out world; we can celebrate "All Things Bright and Beautiful"[5] and look on the bright side. We can join hands with Mr. Rogers, who has provided a very positive outlook for children in his neighborhood. It is interesting to note that he was a Presbyterian minister with some theological training, which must have included an exposure to the thought of John Calvin with his emphasis on original sin and human depravity. I celebrate the shift toward a more positive outlook, one that energizes us to begin our day with hope. Our positive outlook may be a good example that helps others find hope and good solutions to their problems. I want to call attention to Sid Hall's insertion of the word *fundamentally* in that it begins with a hopeful starting point and does not imply that we have no problems in our life journey. Rather, he puts the emphasis where it belongs: there are good places to begin in our stewardship of the universe. That part of the world in which we abide is full of beauty and wonder and invites

---

4. Hall, "Creation Spirituality."

5. A hymn with words by Cecil Frances Alexander (1848) and composed by William Henry Monk (1887).

Creation Spirituality

us to find joyful meaning in the work we do. Yet the problems are very real here on earth. There is an incredible amount of suffering, and we do not know that much about the rest of the universe. We go with a positive mindset but need to be somewhat cautious in our descriptions; we do not really know that "the universe, and all life within it, is a blessing." What we do know is that there are blessings within it.

2. "It is through the work of spiritual practice that we move beyond fear into compassion and discover our deep and true selves."

    I find it very easy to support this second affirmation of creation spirituality. Over time, I have discovered that thoughtful and consistent engagement in spiritual practice is life-changing; it cultivates and nurtures the best that is in us. What was once fear that led us into depression and a negative outlook becomes an acceptance of who we are, a celebration of our gifts, and the belief that we can find a purpose in our lives that is positive and contributes to the common good. It is so liberating to have a positive view of who and what we are, one not clouded by fear and excessive guilt from past experience. Yet there is some risk in misguided and exaggerated opinions of ourselves as brilliant, totally healthy, ethical, and able to accomplish nearly anything. Such a view may be rooted in the need to overcome our poor self-image and a not too subtle request for attention and admiration. I have been profoundly helped by engaging in mindful spiritual practices and continue to need them to sustain and continue my growth toward health and maturity.[6]

3. "The spiritual journey can be understood as a dance moving in and out of four mystical paths:

    - Awe, delight, gratitude, joy (known as *Via Positiva*)
    - Uncertainty, darkness, suffering, letting go (known as *Via Negativa*)
    - Birthing, creativity, passion (known as *Via Creativa*)
    - Justice, healing, celebration, rebirth, resurrection (known as *Via Tranformativa*)."

    This essential component of creation spirituality does speak to the many dimensions of personhood. I do once again affirm these positive *dances*, but know that they are aspirations and that few of us attain

---

6. See my book *Mindful Spirituality: The Intentional Cultivation of the Spiritual Life.*

their full expression in our lives. It is a journey, and many of us are just getting started. As we review the positive values and experiences of the four mystical paths, we can honestly say that they wonder-full. Yet it is difficult not to be a wallflower; we do need the presence of other mature people; we do not exclusively dance alone. Being guided by mature people and life-giving groups with our growth and development at the center of their care for us is absolutely essential. Further, many of us as leaders and counselors find it difficult not to be at least partially driven by our own needs. To have these needs is a given; to be controlled by them in our healing work with others is a risk. We grow together when there is compassion and truth, love and light. I want also to underline the dimension of *via negativa* in this expression and suggested dance of creation spirituality. It is important to find and affirm the positive as we express the elements of the spiritual journey. Yet to not fully understand the harsh reality and power of evil and the overwhelming nature of the world's problems would invite us into a false perception of the condition of our world and the profound challenges we face. It is hard to dance to a tune based on false assumptions.

4. "Every one of us carries within us the capacity to be a mystic, to be creative, to be visionary, and to be an agent of positive change. It is our responsibility to cultivate these capacities for the benefit of Earth and all of its creatures."

    I strongly affirm the intention of this goal. I do sincerely hope that most of us have these qualities, and to state this essential component in this way is to encourage us to draw them out, cultivate them, and express them. But, not unlike the other essential components listed, I find myself wanting to qualify it and ask for clarity regarding its intention. It may be more of a noble aspiration than an omnipresent reality. Some gifted people may have the capacity to be a mystic, to be creative, to be a visionary, and to contribute to improving life for all, but not everyone. In fact, it may be that there are only a limited percentage of people who have a full portion of these qualities. Might there be some wisdom in saying that the goal of creation spirituality is to encourage all of us who have these inherent qualities in varying levels to cultivate them and to use them for the benefit of the Earth and all of its creatures?

5. "We rejoice in and courageously honor the rich diversity within the Cosmos which is expressed in every religious and ancestral tradition."

Creation Spirituality

I strongly affirm this essential component in creation spirituality, especially in reference to inclusivity and the risk when it is not present. For example, I have been active for a number of years in the Christian church, and it has been quite common to find within nearly every branch and denomination an exclusive component in both belief and practice. As time went along, as I read more, and as I traveled in many countries of the world, I discovered that it was difficult to maintain that Christianity is the only true religion and that the other religions are wrong in their beliefs and in some cases do not have the correct ethical guidelines. Gradually I began to discover in every religion that both beliefs and practices tend to emerge out of our time and place in history and through our language and culture. I realized that I was a Protestant Christian, nurtured in my faith in an American context, and taught from a Reformed perspective. That was what I was exposed to and taught by good and gifted people. I remain, although with growth across the years, within the Christian family and in Christian communities that are linked to the Reformed tradition. It has and will likely continue to be my spiritual home. I have learned, however, that it would not be wise to make this tradition the only way to connect with the Divine.

I now realize that God comes to us at the point and level of our understanding. God speaks many languages and we listen with our language and mindset. We use the symbols and metaphors of our language and culture to put our faith together. What I saw as I was exposed to other religions was the ways their beliefs and practices express what is appropriate and nurturing for their people. I also began to realize that much of our theology is approximation and does not fully express the full reality of Transcendence. God comes to meet us within the limitations of our time and place in history, and we use our tradition, language, education, and culture to express our religious belief. Our environment conditions our understanding and descriptions of our beliefs and practices; they are not absolute truth, but relative to our time and place. We may have a good way of understanding Transcendence and the values that are a true expression of the divine will and way, but we can also rejoice that we see it in other religious traditions as well. We see more clearly when we note our own failures to live up to the expression of truth in our tradition. We can correct it, and begin to consistently express love, compassion, and the quest for justice.

6. "Ecological and social justice are our priority as imperatives for the healing, sustainability, and harmony among our species and the entire Earth community."

Once again, I fully support this statement and have no doubt that as conditions in the world change that the statement will continue to be nuanced; in fact it is carefully nuanced in Sid Hall's writing. I would only add that so much happens so fast, as for example COVID-19; there is constant change. Therefore, we will need to continually update our expression of this deep commitment and to be tangible and specific in how we give attention to other global problems that are not easily categorized as environmental and social justice. Further, it is important to fully describe what is needed in these categories of environmental and social justice. It is all too easy, for example, to neglect the role and treatment of women when we exclusively focus our attention on racial justice.

I am profoundly grateful for the emergence of creation spirituality in our common life. It has helped me to rearrange the way I put faith together. It has not taken away my faith and my understanding of the nature of my spiritual journey, but has enhanced them both. Although it has challenged some basic understandings of Christian thought and practice, it has not so much removed them as it has informed them and invited the Christian family, and indeed all who seek a spiritual way, to reconfigure belief and practice in a way that incorporates the best insights of current thought and to follow a spiritual pathway that is fully engaged with the contemporary world.

We sense that there is a trace of Transcendence when we gaze at the beauty and complexity of nature and the emergence of humankind and understand it as original blessing; it may more accurately reflect the divine way than the doctrine of original sin. The correction of the overly negative view reflected in the cosmic fall of humankind that we see in creation spirituality may give us better sight of how Transcendence and transcendence may be at work in the evolution of the human race.

THE INTEGRATION OF SCIENCE AND RELIGION

We are exploring the ways that we who live in the modern and postmodern world have undertaken the quest to understand and connect with Transcendence. One of the assumptions that undergird this quest is that we need to bring the great insights from the premodern world into our world with its modern and now postmodern (global and planetary) worldview. How do Buddha and Jesus speak to our time? The translation of their universal beliefs and practices must be done with great care in order to be true to their wisdom, yet make this wisdom available in a credible and life-giving way. There have been a multitude of approaches to this challenge, and one that we just considered is creation spirituality. We read the ancient and founding literature with sound historical-critical methods and hermeneutical wisdom. We try to bring universal wisdom, present in very time-limited containers, forward into our way of understanding the world, sensitive to our contemporary understanding of nature and human history. Creation spirituality was introduced as illustrative of this quest. We now turn to one other way this hermeneutical quest has been undertaken, that of integrating spiritual wisdom with a scientific understanding of the world. We know that the world was not created is six days.

THE THOUGHT OF PIERRE TEILHARD DE CHARDIN

Around the world and especially in Europe, there were tremendous changes and increased diversity during the late eighteenth century, through the nineteenth century, and into the twentieth century in religious thought and practice. The starting points, ideas, and methods of understanding that developed in the Enlightenment entered into the intense discussion of the how it is that we gain knowledge. We dip into this critical conversation on one edge as we continue our study of how it is that we find and understand traces of Transcendence. From the Enlightenment came liberation from the authority of tradition; it was literally a Copernican revolution. The earth was not the center of the universe, but a distant and small planet in a vast galaxy. Mindsets had to change.

In the European context, the church used its accumulated authority to dictate what we should believe about the world. The belief systems tended to be earth centered and dealt almost exclusively with the human drama

Section Two: The Modern Quest to Understand and Connect with Transcendence

But with a careful look into a telescope, this understanding was challenged, and with it came the scientific method as the way of learning and knowing.

It was not too long after the dramatic changes in scientific inquiry that a similar challenge came in understanding history. The basic tools of scientific inquiry moved over to historical understanding, and, of course, this way of knowing turned to the Bible and the literal reading of Genesis, with its myth of a six-day creation, and the life and teaching of Jesus, the primary subject of Christian belief. Whether the Bible's accounts are literally true or more the products of a pre-scientific age in a specific culture became a major topic of discussion and a challenge to traditional Christian belief. This inquiry has had a long period of heated debate and even continues into the present.

Many thoughtful scholars challenged the way that belief systems were articulated in a classical and traditional way. Attempts were made to find a way of accepting a scientific understanding of the created world and to apply a historical-critical method to reading the Bible. It was in this context that Pierre Teilhard de Chardin (1881–1955) lived and undertook his calling in life. He was born in Paris and his education had many dimensions. It included philosophy and theology as he studied for the priesthood, and he was ordained as a priest in 1911 and entered the Jesuit order. He also continued his study of geology and paleontology as he pursued his special interest in evolution. He received his doctorate in paleontology at the Sorbonne. He lived in Europe during the First World War and saw human tragedy firsthand as a stretcher-bearer. He was awarded the Legion of Honor for his dedicated service in the war.

Following his education and military service, he chose to go to China as a missionary and to do research in paleontology, tasks that he undertook from 1923 to 1946. The focus of his research was mammalian evolution. As he continued his research, he began to see a larger frame of reference in which to understand human life. He wrote about these observations in a theological frame of reference in two well-known books, *The Phenomenon of Man* and *The Divine Milieu*, but the Catholic Church did not allow their publication. Many years later, he moved to New York to continue his work and these two books and several others, including *The Appearance of Man*, were published following his death.

In his writing, he addressed no less a subject than a universal view of the world and human existence. As he gazed at and studied the world through his scientific frame of reference and reflected on what he saw through the perspective of his faith, he began to develop a way to overcome the differences between these two perspectives and to bring them together in a common worldview. As a geologist, he studied the various levels of rocks and understood them as layers of time and evolutionary development. He then noted another sphere or level beyond the inanimate, that of life in plants and forests, and began to see different spheres, moving from inanimate matter, the geosphere, to biological matter, the biosphere. In time, following an evolutionary pattern, he noted another step in the evolutionary process, namely, that early humanoids began to use reason to see the connections between cause and effect. There were early forms of consciousness and the use of very basic language that enabled communication and emotional linkage with others. Teilhard called this sphere the *noosphere* (*nous* meaning mind in Greek) and saw the socialization of humankind as an evolutionary pattern, one that might point to a transcendent purpose guided by a divine mind. With many steps in between, based on years of research, Teilhard began to reflect on the meaning of this evolutionary pattern. Drawing upon his Christian faith, he pointed to Jesus as the end goal of human development, an *Omega Point*. He goes on in his reflections to suggest that this final development, the Christ event, will become the *Parousia* or Second Coming. In faith, he speaks of the Omega Point as the ultimate purpose of evolutionary development, now carried on in human history by the church and the range of advanced human organizations that engage in creating a humane and just world. In his other writings, he more fully develops this end goal of evolution. Although mistrusted by the Church and criticized by many of his scientific colleagues, Teilhard's vision of integrating a theological outlook with modern science is an important contribution as humans reflect on how it is all connected.

THE VISION OF ILIA DELIO

Illio Delio is a Franciscan sister and professor at Villanova University. She has advanced degrees in both theology and science, and has made the thought of Pierre Teilhard de Chardin a major focus in her teaching and writing. She has a deep interest in evolution, physics, and neuroscience and has used these specialties as she continues the task that was central to the work of Teilhard, that of integrating or at least finding common ground between science and theology. She is the author of twenty books, including *The Unbearable Wholeness of Being: God, Evolution and the Power of*

Section Two: The Modern Quest to Understand and Connect with Transcendence

Love (2013), *Making All Things New: Catholicity, Cosmology, Consciousness* (2015), and *The Emergent Universe: Exploring the Meaning of Catholic in an Evolutionary Universe* (2011). In her extensive writing, she gives thoughtful attention to the following topics:

- She begins on a personal note and reflects on how she found God in everyone and everywhere, a discovery that transformed her life. For her, God is very present in all that exists. It is her starting point. She learned from Immanuel Kant that "two things fill the mind with ever new and increasing wonder and awe, the starry heaven above me and the moral law within me."[7]

- She speaks about how the universe may be thought of as a new monastery, one in which we find deep and profound meaning as we learn to love the creation and all of its creatures. This conviction becomes her inspiration, motivation, and purpose in life. She invites us to join with God in the ongoing processes of creation.

- She speaks about the quest for wholeness, a quest that becomes a basic dimension in human life, and likens it to the life of the universe, beginning with the big bang, the movement from the inanimate to the rise of consciousness and the journey of love. We join with God in helping and empowering everything and especially humans to become all that God intends for them to be.

- She reflects on current developments in the formation of the earth and the evolution of humankind. Progress has been made, yet there is much more to come. She underlines the advancement of artificial intelligence (AI) as a pathway forward, moving toward "ecological re-enchantment of the earth."

- And, as a foundational conviction of her thought, she writes that, "Life is not an established structure but a work of art in which the work itself includes the imagination of God and the serendipity of nature in an ongoing creative process."[8]

There is certainly a strong Roman Catholic flavor to the thought and writing of both Teilhard and Delio, yet a warm and welcoming one for those outside of the Roman Catholic tradition. Both of these authors are cosmic

---

7. Kant, *Critique of Practical Reason*, quoted by Pelikan, *Christian Doctrine and Modern Culture*, 118.

8. Delio, *Birth of the Dancing Star*, 187.

and inclusive in their outlook and view the creation and all of its many parts and dimensions as revelatory and an expression of God's love. In fact, their emphasis on understanding the universe and showing compassion to all of its many dimensions reminds one of the person who has inspired them, Jesus. As the Gospel of John reminds us, Jesus was "full of grace and truth" (1:14). It is grace and truth that are the traces of Transcendence and must be present as we live in troubled times and seek to understand the universe and care about its future.

6

Contemplative Spirituality
The Ways of Introspection and Meditation

TURNING INWARD

WE HAVE BEEN USING directional metaphors to describe the ways that the human family has sought and found spiritual pathways that empower them to cope with life's severe problems and to flourish, ones that enable a life filled with meaning, joy, and serenity. In the first section of our study, we considered spiritual pathways in the premodern world that *looked outward* to nature and history as a way of understanding and linking with Transcendence. It was nature and history that taught them how to understand life, to live wisely, and to shape their own history. We then considered premodern spiritual pathways that *looked inward* to find Transcendence or a profound insight or principle that gave order and structure to their surroundings and to their lives. They sought to discover a pathway or single principle or Presence (monism) that would enlighten them and enable them both to cope with a dangerous world and to find peace and meaning in that endeavor. We then turned our attention to those premodern religions in the Abrahamic monotheistic tradition that *looked upward* to connect and be reconciled with Transcendence, the Divine, or God.

In Section Two, we are exploring modern spiritual pathways, giving attention once again to directional metaphors that at least partially describe their essence. We looked first at two contemporary spiritual pathways that tend to look outward toward creation and history to find a spiritual direction. Matthew Fox, a Catholic theologian, has guided with great depth and clarity a movement called *creation spirituality*. The central theme of this orientation is that creation is God's blessing and gift and invites those seeking spiritual guidance to look positively at the good creation and their lives as full of potential for meaning and peace of mind. We then turned our attention to a way of integrating the evolutionary developmental character of history, science, and faith, looking at the thought of Pierre Teilhard de Chardin and Illia Delio. Teilhard did his work primarily in China in the early to mid twentieth century, and Delio's work is a contemporary invitation to celebrate and devote one's life to the ongoing evolutionary processes of creation.

We turn now to modern spiritual pathways that tend to *look inward* to find spiritual direction and guidance. Our goal is to understand how the great religious traditions of the human family, such as Buddhism, Hinduism, and their many cousins, have turned inward in modern times to understand and find their connection with Transcendence, Presence, and Source. These grand traditions are seeking to find faithful and authentic ways to link their beliefs and practices with the contemporary world. Their goal is to help their adherents to understand how the profound insights of their religious traditions about life might jump forward into the present world to guide and nurture their contemporary adherents, helping them to awaken and become enlightened. It is no small task.

THE WAY OF BUDDHISM

We turn to the life and thought of some of the most significant modern leaders and teachers of the spiritual way of Buddhism in order to discern patterns of belief and practice that bring the heart of Buddhism into the contemporary world. I have selected three individuals from a vast array of influential people within the Buddhist tradition: the Dalai Lama, Thich Nhat Hanh, and Pema Chödrön.[1] The Dalai Lama, of course, has had a profound influence well beyond his place of residence in North India helping and guiding people around the world. The same may be said of the Vietnamese teacher and monk Thich Nhat Hanh, who was forced to

---

1. Scott A. Mitchell, in his recent book *Buddhism in America: Global Religion, Local Contexts*, provides a thoughtful description of the way that Buddhism is adapted to different settings in the contemporary world.

leave Vietnam during the war and settled in a monastery in France. Pema Chödrön, a dedicated Buddhist nun and leader of a retreat center in Nova Scotia, has focused her teaching and writing on the practical application of Buddhist thought, the way of the Bodhisattva.

All three of these gifted teachers have assumed in their writing that the reader will have a basic understanding of what is often taught as the foundation of Buddhism, the Four Noble Truths and the Eightfold Path. I will list these teachings for reference as we look at the way these three teachers have shaped the practice of contemporary Buddhism.

The Four Noble Truths:

1. Life is filled with suffering; human sorrow is universal.
2. The suffering and sorrow are caused by attachment and craving; we have an insatiable desire to have and possess.
3. The Buddha teaches that there is a way to overcome and end this suffering.
4. It is to become enlightened and to live by and follow the Eightfold Path.

The Eightfold Path includes:

1. The right view, or having the right understanding of reality and to be guided by the truth, avoiding all forms of delusion.
2. The right intention, to have the best motivation and be free from ignorance and self-centeredness as we set goals.
3. The right speech, using appropriate language to express wisdom, truth, and enlightenment.
4. The right action, to practice what we preach, to act with integrity, and to be a healing presence.
5. The right livelihood, to seek a way of making a living that is in keeping with Buddhist values.
6. The right effort, to nurture our beliefs and practices in a way that sustains a healthy pattern of life.
7. Right mindfulness, cultivating and nurturing a consciousness that keeps us living in the present and on track.
8. Right concentration, or staying focused on the beliefs and practices of our faith orientation.

Each of these components of the Eightfold path is related to the other, giving a unified and comprehensive vision of the good life.

THE DALAI LAMA

We turn first to the Dalai Lama, who has had a worldwide influence. I want us to reflect on his way of life and his teaching, both of which have inspired so many and given insight about how to pattern one's life in a way that leads to health and happiness. He was born in Tibet and, early in his youth, he was carefully chosen by the religious community into which he was born as one who had a particular calling, a true vocation to become the Dalia Lama, the leader of Tibetan Buddhism. As a young boy, he experienced with his Tibetan religious family the persecution of the Chinese government, which had taken over the nation of Tibet. One goal of the Chinese government was, as far as possible, to eliminate religion, and it became apparent that the young and chosen future leader of Tibetan Buddhism was in danger. He did escape from Tibet and settled in the somewhat isolated and lovely town of Dharamsala in Northern India. It is from this setting that he has been able to undertake his two primary goals in life. The first is to bring health and happiness to individual seekers, regardless of their religious orientation, who suffer and need help and healing. His second goal has been to join with others around the world in helping to create a more just and humane world.

In his book *The Art of Happiness: A Handbook for Living*, one of many that might have been chosen, he, with Dr. Howard C. Cutler, speak about the way that individuals can find a way to overcome their mental and emotional suffering, get on the road to enlightenment, and find deep and joyful inner peace.[2] The book covers the following topics: in Part I, the authors address the purpose of life; Part II, the place of human warmth and intimacy; Part III, the way of transforming suffering; Part IV, how to overcome obstacles to happiness; and Part V, closing reflections on living the spiritual life as the pathway to health and happiness.

In Part I, the Dalai Lama with his coauthor, a psychiatrist, speak first about the right to happiness and to maintain that state of mind regardless of one's religion or lack of it; all people are seeking a happy and fulfilled life. It is the direction of every life, although for a variety of reasons, both

---

2. The book *The Art of Happiness* was written with an American doctor, Howard C. Cutler, and published in 1998. Its insights and wisdom are timeless, and its time of publication does not suggest that its message is any less germane now than it was in 1998.

Section Two: The Modern Quest to Understand and Connect with Transcendence

personal and cultural, human beings tend to get lost, in part because they make poor choices and in part because the environment in which they live denies them the opportunity to find happiness. The two authors maintain that a majority of the world's population has subscribed to false promises: that happiness consists of satisfying one's ego needs, that happiness consists in the abundance of things possessed, and that happiness comes when we have power and control over others. Both the Dalai Lama and Dr. Cutler illustrate from their own lives and from research that these falsehoods need to be overcome and to realize that we achieve true happiness by becoming aware of and use the true sources of happiness.

The fundamental foundation of happiness is a function of "how we perceive our situation, how satisfied we are with what we have."[3] It is our mental state rather than external circumstances that leads to happiness. One's state of mind is the key, although this should not be confused with an apathetic or passive state of mind or not being intentional about pursuing the goal of happiness. One must have both understanding and motivation to find inner contentment. It comes to us as we cultivate a state of consciousness that understands that we need to be grateful for what we have and accept our current circumstances. It is to be conscious of our inner worth as a human being and to live in a supportive human community that gives rise to and supports our sense of worth and dignity. They note as well that although we may have experiences that lead to pleasure, pleasure in itself is not happiness.

As one might expect, the next observation that our authors make is that we must cultivate a positive state of mind. The first step in this cultivation is to learn that negative emotions and behaviors are harmful to us and that we need to understand why they occur and how we can overcome them.[4] Causality is accepted in Buddhism, and one needs to understand and directly face the causes of discomfort and make changes. The second step, of course, is to find good pathways to a healthy way of life and then to use mental discipline as a way of becoming positive in our state of mind. The Dalai Lama underlines the importance of *dharma* in the exercise of

---

3. Dalai Lama and Cutler, *Art of Happiness*, 22.

4. See the book by Jack Kornfield *The Wise Heart: A Guide to the Universal Teachings of Buddhist Psychology* for an excellent treatment of how to overcome conscious and unconscious causes of emotional illness and suffering and then move toward health and wholeness. He has also written another helpful book, *No Time Life the Present: Finding Freedom, Love, and Joy Right Where You Are*, on the theme finding health and happiness in cultivating a deep spirituality.

mental discipline, which is understood as the teachings and doctrine of Buddha. He and Dr. Cutler say that these universal teachings are in harmony with the way that the brain works, and as we incorporate them into our lives we will move toward peace and happiness.

One also achieves happiness and deep satisfaction by being intentional about living an ethical life, a way of life that has integrity with one's deepest values. It is to understand which values are linked to our development and fulfillment as humans and then to make these values the cornerstone of our ethical life. Values such as justice and compassion are on this list, and we need to develop patterns of life and habits that nurture these practices and make them the very foundation of our lives. Here again it is a matter of practice, and as these values guide us in our behavior we are on the road to rediscovering and reclaiming our innate state of happiness. For the Dalai Lama, it is accepting our Buddha nature, that state of mind that is untainted by negative emotions or thoughts and undergirded by a positive and hopeful state of mind. It is to awaken the Buddha within.[5]

The Dalai Lama is conscious of the fact that this positive understanding of human nature that a happy and fulfilled life is possible has been criticized as naïve. He recognizes that it is not always accepted as a fundamental truth of human development. In fact, this optimistic view has not been widely accepted, and reference is made to the views of philosophers such as Hume, scientists such as Charles Darwin, and psychologists such as Freud who have had a more negative outlook on human nature. Yet he affirms that to act selfishly and violently is not inherited and programmed into human nature, but a way that is learned. Other ways of life may be learned as well, such as experiencing personal joy and having a concern for social justice. These qualities are more fundamental to who we are as human beings. It is this positive direction that should be understood as our purpose in life.

In Part II, the authors move to the place of human love in the quest for health and happiness. They speak about the fact that many people, surrounded by others, are still quite lonely, and they attribute this condition to the lack of intimacy. The Dalai Lama notes that he seldom experiences loneliness and maintains that it is because of the way he tries to focus in relationships on what is positive and attractive in those he meets, and that this attitude creates a feeling of affinity with them. It reduces the level of fear or apprehension and increases an openness and trust. He also emphasizes that this positive approach tends to increase his compassion for

---

5. See Lama Surya Das's book *Awakening the Buddha Within*.

others. Rather than fear of rejection or a preoccupation with differences and potential conflict, there is sense of acceptance and identification with others and a natural linkage for sharing and caring at a deeper level. This intimacy promotes physical and psychological well-being. The genuine and deep bonds of sharing one's common humanity help to create a profound sense of belonging; being with others helps us face the profound challenges of human life. The Dalai Lama explains that we are made for one another and therefore need to deepen our connection to others. The foundation of this connection is the feeling of empathy, being able to identify and genuinely care about the journey of others and have them care about your journey as well.

The sense of identification and connection with others, rooted in genuine empathy, leads to compassion, a state of mind that is non-violent, non-harming, and non-aggressive. It is a mental state based on our wish for others to be free from suffering and a commitment and responsibility to act on their behalf, assisting them to overcome all that threatens their well-being. Compassion is not always easy to express in that it calls on us to cease being preoccupied with our own needs and concerns and to selflessly reach out to help others. Again, both the Dalai Lama and Dr. Cutler underline that our capacity to be compassionate requires that we prepare ourselves and cultivate a compassionate state of mind. This means that we will need to incorporate spiritual practices such as meditation into our lives so that we can more easily and naturally reach out to others without mixed motivation and genuinely care for them.

Part III addresses this need to cultivate the capacity to transform the suffering of others. The authors begin with the observation, deeply rooted in the Buddhist tradition, that all human beings suffer at some level and that this reality must be faced directly. Further, Buddhist teaching strongly affirms that there is a way of overcoming our suffering. A first step is to carefully discern the difference between the suffering that is an integral part of our existence and what comes from our own foolish and selfish behavior. We need to accept that there will be a measure of suffering within us that is part of the human condition and that is caused by external circumstances over which we have no control. There is also a measure of suffering we bring on to ourselves by our state of mind, attitudes, and behavior that go against our deepest values. Each of these types of suffering can be addressed. The key to managing the suffering that is an integral part of being human can best be addressed by an honest acceptance of the realities of human life.

Contemplative Spirituality

We get sick, meet people who treat us unfairly, live in unjust and abusive settings, and get old and infirm. There is a sort of stoical dimension in the Buddhist tradition that suggests that these realities in life are best managed by facing them directly and cultivating a state of mind that accepts and manages these realities in a spiritual way. The capacity to accept them without being thrown off balance comes as we engage in spiritual practices that lead to a sense of inner contentment. They also point to ways that these conditions may educate us on how to cope with suffering in mature ways.

There is also a great deal of suffering that we may bring onto ourselves as we fall back into our craving for ego gratification, possessions, and power over others. Again, it is integrating the teaching of Buddha into our lives, welcoming the support that comes from our community, and our centeredness and integrity with our values that guide us in dealing with suffering.

We also have the responsibility to reach out to others and help them with their suffering. With empathy and presence, being there for others, we ease the suffering of those who come into our circle of nearness As the Dalai Lama has, we also face oppressive social conditions that cause human suffering, and with wisdom, energy, and commitment we attempt to change unjust laws and social conditions that create poverty, persecution, and all forms of suffering.

This outlook leads to Part IV in the book, which addresses the obstacles we face as we seek to reduce and eliminate the suffering of others. Bringing about change is not easy; there will be those who have a vested interest in sustaining traditions and practices, often because these traditional ways bring wealth to a privileged few and sustain a comfortable way of life for those in power. Inevitably, as we engage in social change, we will encounter anger and even hatred. As we encounter this resistance, we must learn to respond with understanding and an attempt to reach across boundaries that separate us from others who feel the strong need to defend their beliefs and practices.

In Part V, the Dalai closes his reflections of the art of happiness and reviews the need to be intentional about cultivating the spiritual life. With the foundation of inner contentment, wisdom, and perseverance, we stay with our objective of making life better for others. This can be done as we maintain our deep commitment to our spiritual values.

In several other books, the Dalai Lama has carefully articulated these spiritual and ethical values that are integral to the Buddhist way and how he envisions a way for the historical values and practices of Buddhism to be brought forward and applied to the contemporary world. A few years ago, as the world moved into a new millennium, the Dalai Lama, in part in response to his reception of the Nobel Peace Prize, wrote about the values that should be foundational for the human family. His book *Ethics for the New Millennium* provided a thoughtful foundation for the human community as it entered the twenty-first century.[6] In this volume, he once again underlines his usual starting point and provides a theological-philosophical foundation for ethical behavior. He returns to his understanding of modern society and the need to provide a social structure that empowers and enables human beings to find happiness and fulfillment. He acknowledges the difficulties, restates his orientation to values, and reasserts the goal to provide a setting that is just and humane. Such a setting should have the following ethical norms:

1. the ethic of restraint, encouraging positive values, yet also discouraging behavior that is harmful;

2. the ethic of virtue, the practice of what one believes about truth and justice;

3. the ethic of compassion, wisely helping those in need;

4. the ethic to reduce suffering, the common condition of all human beings;

5. the ethic of discernment, to sense what is a wise course of action that will lead to a better world.

Each of these foundational values is defined and given direction for implementation. He then moves on to describe what he hopes will be the character of the societies of the twenty-first century. With care and a profound sense of the human condition, he makes the following observations:

1. The societies that emerge in the new millennium must be committed to being responsible to the whole world, not exclusively focused on regional and local responsibility.

2. There must be deep and profound levels of commitment on the part of those who lead and guide these new and renewed societies. Again, he acknowledges that there will be regional and local concerns and likely some resistance to uniting with others in the creation of a more

---

6. Dalai Lama, *Ethics for the New Millennium*.

just and compassionate world. But he is clearly global and inclusive in his outlook.

3. These new and renewed societies must be grounded in a compassionate ethical foundation. They must not be driven by a self-serving focus on their own concerns as, for example, they deal with climate change It is a global issue.

4. These new and renewed societies must be committed to peace and disarmament.

5. And these new and renewed societies need not be afraid to draw upon the best values of the religious traditions that have undergirded them. He conditions this goal by acknowledging the way religious traditions have often been narrow, tribal, sectarian, and exclusive, but the best values of these traditions are rooted in a commitment to improve the human condition.

6. His final appeal, with great awareness of the competitive and exclusive nature of most governments, is that these new and renewed societies must be motivated by universal love and compassion.

THICH NHAT HANH

Another inspiring and influential voice in bringing Buddhist thought into the contemporary world is the Vietnamese monk Thich Nhat Hanh. He was active in seeking peace during the long war in his country, and in time, because of danger, he moved to Plum Village, a center for Buddhist thought and meditation in the south of France. Across the past several decades, he has been prolific author, an insightful poet, and a dedicated human rights activist, joining on occasion with the Dalai Lama in conferences and social justice initiatives. I want to focus on those writings devoted to two of his most cherished values, love and peace.

In his book *Teachings of Love*, he begins by providing a description of love by turning to Buddhist thought. He uses the Four Immeasurable Minds as a way of defining love. These are:

1. *Maîtiri*: lovingkindness, the desire to offer happiness;

2. *Karuna*: compassion, the desire to remove suffering from the other person;

3. *Mudita*: joy, the desire to bring joy to others and enable their happiness;
4. *Upeksha*: equanimity, the desire to accept reality and be at peace and then to teach this value and way of life to others.

He writes: "If we learn ways to practice love, compassion, joy, and equanimity, we will know how to heal the illnesses of anger, sorrow, insecurity, loneliness, and unhealthy attachments."[7] He moves on directly to how it is that we cultivate these characteristics of love in our lives. He stresses the fact that loving others is not always easy, especially loving those who are not attractive and whose behavior is offensive and harmful. We must be empowered to love, that is, we must prepare ourselves through spiritual practices and then commit ourselves to understanding the need for love. He also notes that self-love is necessary in order to love others in that if we are unsure of our value and have profound needs, we will not be free to express true love to others. We will be preoccupied with our own needs and self-reference all that is said to us; we will not be able to extend ourselves into the lives of others and show genuine empathy.

In fact, those of us who have reached a certain level of maturity and happiness are then free to truly love another, to understand others, and to care for them in wise and healing ways. These ways include deep listening and loving speech, being mindful and fully present for those in our midst, and being able to forgive and begin anew. He underscores five mindfulness trainings as part of our needed understanding about human suffering and the need to love those who suffer:

- Be aware of the suffering caused by the destruction of life in war; it is these people who grieve and need love and understanding.
- Be aware of the suffering caused by exploitation, social injustice, stealing, and oppression. Many people live in settings where there is no love and compassion and little opportunity to rise above one's harmful circumstances.
- Be aware of the suffering caused by sexual misconduct. Thich Nhat Hanh has been especially aware of the abuse of women as he saw the ravages of war in his country.
- Be aware of the suffering caused by unmindful speech and the inability to listen to others. Many people are lonely because they have no one to speak with in an honest and caring way.

7. Hanh, *Teachings on Love*, 3. He has recently passed away.

- And be aware of the suffering caused by excessive consumption. He speaks directly about the risks of alcohol and drug use.

He concludes his book on the teachings of love by underlining the importance of having a supportive community where one is respected and welcomed.[8]

In addition to his writing on love, Thich Nhat Hanh has also brought his Buddhist faith to his understanding of the terrible damage of war and the quest for peace. His treatment of this theme has been profound and extensive and goes well beyond our discussion, but I do want to stress one dimension of his thoughts about peace, one that is always present in his writing: it is the living of these values that is important, not just the discussion about them. In his book *Being Peace*, the title itself underlines his understanding of the nature of peace. In this small volume of selected essays, Thich Nhat Hanh speaks about the nature of peace and stresses that we need to understand the causes of war and conflict, learn how to build a more just and compassionate society and world, and engage in cultivating peace by the quality of our lives and how we use our talent and resources. He provides observations about the causes of conflict and war and suggests that peace will come from global change, of course, but also by us "being peace," that is, dedicating our lives to join with others in creating peace. Peace must be present in the smaller domains of our everyday life as well as in the corporate structures of our communities, countries, and the world.

PEMA CHÖDRÖN

I want to introduce one other contemporary teacher of Buddhist thought and practice, Pema Chödrön, in part because she is able to speak in such a profound way about the special concerns of women and also because, in her role as American Buddhist nun, she speaks directly to her American readers about the need for reorienting their lives and the practical application of Buddhist teachings. The titles of her books prior to one we are considering, *No Time to Lose: The Way of the Bodhisattva*, provide us with some understanding of how carefully she has applied the classic patterns of thought and practice of Buddhism to the contemporary world with all of its challenging conditions. The titles are: *The Wisdom of No Escape, Start*

---

8. An especially helpful book on love by Thich Nhat Hanh is entitled *How to Love*, and in this small volume he provides counsel on how to cultivate a life of love.

Section Two: The Modern Quest to Understand and Connect with Transcendence

Where You Are, When Things Fall Apart, The Places that Scare You, Comfortable with Uncertainty, and *The Compassionate Box.*

In *No Time to Lose*, in a very insightful and informative way, she brings the ancient teachings of how to follow the way of Bodhisattva (one in training to follow the Buddhist Way) into the present. She uses the classic text *The Way of the Bodhisattva*, which was composed in India by Shantideva, a Buddhist monk, over twelve centuries ago. Her exegesis and hermeneutical strategy make this writing remarkably relevant for all of us who are seeking a deeper spirituality, one that empowers us to live a constructive life in the contemporary world. Initially, in the introduction to the book, Pema Chödrön acknowledges that it is a difficult task and that she lacks the necessary experience to guide others who want to follow the way of the Bodhisattva. But her humility, in my judgment, makes her presentation even more persuasive. She struggles with ways to have integrity with her religious beliefs as I do, and she is far more advanced in this quest that I am!

She has provided contemporary titles to each section of the book, ones that provide the reader with a clear behavioral value and how it might be incorporated into the lives of those who seek to be a true Bodhisattva. Her title, *No Time to Lose*, underscores what she believes to be crucial for the spiritual pilgrim who can make a difference in our troubled world; get started now with the clear intention of awakening to the sacred. She quotes from *The Way of the Bodhisattva*:

> And now as long as space endures,
> As long as there are beings to be found,
> May I continue likewise to remain
> To drive away the sorrow of the world.[9]

She continues her exposition and exegesis of *The Way* and draws upon the Eightfold Path by expressing the need for all pilgrims to develop a clear intention, one patterned after the awakened heart of the Bodhisattva. She underlines the "Three Jewels of Buddhism," the Buddha (the model), the *dharma* (the teaching), and the *sangha* (the community), as the sources for developing the right intention. She writes about how this classic teaching, now twelve hundred years in the past, teaches the Bodhisattva how to prepare the ground for the cultivation of the dedicated life. She notes that the pilgrim will inevitably encounter doubts that cause one to be hesitant to go forward; the task is very demanding.

---

9. Verse 10.55 in *The Way*, quoted in Chödrön, *No Time to Lose*, xvii.

But there are excellent resources available that enable us to overcome the obstacles and most basic is the wise use of our intelligence (it is there for a reason). This will require the taming of the mind and the practice of vigilance. With this foundation, one can proceed on the Way by not causing harm to others, gathering and cultivating key virtues of the Buddha's teaching, and engaging in behavior that benefits others. As one proceeds on this path, there will be some frustration, such as the rise of anger, calling for the inner disciplines of patience, enthusiasm, and heroic perseverance. The Bodhisattva must realize that all people must cope with *karma*, that there are consequences for our actions, and with *samsara*, the cycle of death and rebirth. In time, as we are faithful, we can attain our goal.

THE WAYS OF HINDUISM

There are many thoughtful interpreters of Buddhism; in fact it is remarkable how over the last several decades, going back to the mid-twentieth century, Buddhism has been so attractive to spiritual seekers. It has been a very positive development in the United States, Western Europe, and many other parts of the world. There has been a similar resurgence, although perhaps less visible, in various strands of Hindu thought and practice. Yet thoughtful teachers of Hinduism have been able to bring this great religious outlook forward into the lives of people all around the world.[10] They have accomplished the goal of translating the ancient teachings of Hinduism into contemporary language and relevance for our troubled world. One might point to a range of swamis, Hindu religious teachers, who have guided people in the Western world, some who have not always pursued their mission to enlighten others in reputable ways. Yet the guiding beliefs and practices of Hinduism, pointing to a way of understanding Transcendence, continue to provide a positive way to engage in a life-giving spiritual journey. I want to look briefly at two modern, although not contemporary, representatives of Hinduism whose lives and teachings have not only had an influence on their settings, but have touched other parts of the world as well. One great leader within the Hindu tradition, although hardly orthodox in his views, Mohandas Gandhi, may be one of the people on everybody's list of the top ten most influential people of the twentieth century. The other person I am choosing to discuss is more of a philosopher and poet whose life and

---

10. Jeffrey D. Long, in his recent book *Hinduism in America: A Convergence of Worlds*, describes the way that Hinduism has adjusted to a different culture.

thought are less well known, but his influence has been profound and foundational in the formation the intellectual life of India: Sri Aurobindo.

As I attempt to summarize their lives and writing, I am very conscious that a summary may miss the intended meaning, even distort it, and oversimplify subtle thought and the complexity of extraordinary lives. This reality is especially evident as one crosses languages and cultures, speaks as an outsider, attempts to describe religious and philosophical thought, and tries to capture the essence of a great person. I sense this risk as I comment on the lives and thought of Sri Aurobindo and Mohandas Gandhi, yet I hope my brief comments might be suggestive and motivate those with interest to dig deeper and go to the original sources.

AUROBINDO GHOSE

Sri (meaning honorary sir) Aurobindo was born in South India in 1872 and was a distinguished poet, philosopher, and nationalist across the critical years of India's quest for independence. He gave special attention to the foundations of Hindu thought and how it might take shape in the modern world. Educated at Kings College, Cambridge, he returned to Pondicherry, the French region of India, to join in the nationalist cause of India. He was passionate in this cause and was even arrested for writing articles against British rule.

While he devoted his adult life to this nationalist cause, he also began his career in higher education, devoting himself to teaching and writing. Among his many writings was the book entitled *The Life Divine*, a synthesis of yoga, the religious outlook and practice of Hinduism. Brilliant in his analysis, he draws upon the current strands of intellectual inquiry to which he was exposed at Cambridge, and was particularly interested in the thought of Plato, Hegel, Darwin, and his contemporary, Pierre Teilhard de Chardin. He was inspired to work toward integrating their thought and bringing it into harmony with the philosophical foundations of Hindu theology. In particular, drawing upon the Upanishads and the Bhagavad Gita in particular, and using the thought of the great names in Western philosophy from Plato to Kant, he braids together a beautiful synthesis in describing reality. The depth and profundity of his thought has been and continues to be admired as among the finest in modern philosophy.

The foundation of his thought begins with a fundamental truth of Indian thought, that Hinduism allows and encourages it adherents to be free in the pursuit of a meaningful and fulfilled life. He notes that there was no single founder of Hinduism who taught a particular path, as is the case with the Abrahamic monotheistic religions, which look specifically to the teachings of Moses, Jesus, and Muhammad. Nor does he endorse the notion that one must find ways to appease a demanding eternal judge and overcome evil behavior in order to become acceptable and free. Rather, his worldview is rooted in the notion that there is Brahman (Transcendence) that is guiding universal evolution. The presence of the Divine, often called *Supermind* or *Spirit*, is moving evolution forward toward perfection, and it is the role of religion to assist and guide humanity to follow the direction of Spirit in order to reach the goal of pure love and justice for all (the Omega Point in the thought of Teilhard).

The aim and voice of Spirit is speaking through matter, as in evolution; it is matter that reveals the face of Spirit or Supermind, the expression of Brahman, the universal being, understood not as personal, but as the source and energy of the universe. As we get onboard with this fundamental reality, we begin our spiritual journey, and our spiritual practices, based in yoga, will illuminate and enlighten us as we press forward toward the formation of a new world. We are guided to move toward becoming a new species and participate in creating a new world rooted in compassion, justice, and peace.

Aurobindo notes that Darwin described the way of evolution for natural phenomena, but did not describe or explain the reason behind it, which is the movement of Supermind as a manifestation of Brahman. One can trace this movement in the literature of Hinduism, the Vedas in particular, and then make the connection and integration with such great minds as Plato, Hegel, and Teilhard de Chardin. There is a universal consciousness in the process of self-manifestation and self-realization, a point of view that caused Ken Wilbur, the American philosopher, to describe Aurobindo as India's greatest philosopher.

There is so much more that could and perhaps should be said about the life and teachings of Aurobindo, but perhaps this brief introduction will encourage those with interest to read his writing and the expositions of his thought. Suffice to say that he provided for many Indian leaders a philosophical foundation for ways of applying Hinduism to the cultivation of a more just modern India. He articulated the way of Hinduism, the basis of the worldview that undergirds the life and patterns of thought and culture of India, and used its guiding principles to map the formation and development

Section Two: The Modern Quest to Understand and Connect with Transcendence

of modern India. He wrote, regarding his spiritual beliefs and his commitment to the formation of a new India: "Those who say that spirituality has nothing to do with politics do not know what spirituality means."[11]

MAHATMA (GREAT SOUL) GANDHI

Mohandas Gandhi, the great leader of the nationalist cause and the liberation of India, was guided by the thought of Aurobindo as he led India into the future.[12] Gandhi was born in West India in 1869. His father was a government official and Mohandas had opportunities to see several parts of India as his father was transferred from place to place. In their travels, they noted that education was foundational for a good life in India, and his family made sure that he received a good education. When his father died as a relatively young man, Gandhi was sent to England to study law in the hope that he would become a successful modern professional when he returned. Gandhi's wife, who was quite young, joined him on the journey to England. While they enjoyed the time in England, it was not a completely satisfying experience. Both were relatively shy and reserved, and they both felt somewhat removed from the social life of these new surroundings. When Gandhi returned to India, he was not immediately hired and did not move directly into professional life as a lawyer. His English education did not immediately qualify him for a prominent position. However, a position did open up for him in South Africa, one that he thought would last for just a year. When he arrived in South Africa, he soon discovered that there was a clear separation of classes based in large measure on race. In particular, he personally experienced discrimination as an Indian and saw that people of color did not have the same opportunities for education and employment and therefore suffered from poverty. They did not have equal opportunity to pursue a healthy and productive life. He immediately got involved in politics and the quest for social justice, and what was thought to be a yearlong appointment lasted for over two decades. It was this setting and these circumstances that caused Gandhi to become more deeply religious

---

11. Quote by Jack Kornfield in *The Wise Heart*, 352.

12. There are several fine biographies of Gandhi. I have been helped in my understanding of the life and influence of Gandhi by the biography written by his grandson, Rajmohan Gandhi, entitled *Gandhi: The Man, His People, and the Empire*. Judith Brown from Oxford University has edited and published *The Essential Writings*, providing us with a well-edited and thoughtful introduction to Gandhi's writing.

and committed to creating a more humane and just social order. He also emerged as a national figure and began to be noticed as a social reformer in the world context. He became known as a "little saint" that must be taken seriously. Winston Churchill said that it was "nauseating" that "a Middle Temple lawyer now posing as a fakir was striding half-naked up the steps of the viceregal palace to parley on equal terms with the representative of the King-Emperor." Churchill added: "The truth is that Gandhism and all it stands for will have to be grappled with and finally crushed."[13]

He returned to India as a proven leader, and also one who was deeply spiritual with a distinct style and point of view. It wasn't long before he became involved with Indian politics, although he was unlike other politicians in India, both in his point of view and his way of life. For example, he was not an identical twin with the handsome and professional Nehru, his contemporary in the struggle in the nationalist cause in India. He had become a deeply religious person, rooted in the Hindu tradition and influenced by other religious traditions, including Christianity and of course Islam, given the large Islamic population in India that later formed the country of Pakistan.[14] He cooperated and debated with other Indian leaders, but did so as "holy man" with a different dress, lifestyle, and depth of conviction. The political story of the liberation of India from British control is dramatic and complex, and it became understood and influential worldwide. Our focus is to understand how his deep religious convictions, brought forward from great religious traditions of the human family, especially Hinduism, were given modern relevance in a most remarkable way in the twentieth century in India. I want to underline a few these values and principles that were instrumental in the life of Gandhi as he led the transformation of India.

First, in keeping with the Hindu tradition, he devoted himself to becoming the kind of person who would have the convictions and courage to pursue such important and difficult challenges as the liberation of India from colonial rule. These beliefs and convictions were numerous and demanding. I will mention just three:

- He was committed to *bhakti*, perhaps best understood as religious devotion. He gave himself to the practices of Hindu spirituality. He writes about becoming one who will overcome the "chain of ever-recurring birth and death. The only means for this is *bhakti* . . . Without

13. Gandhi, *Gandhi*, 323.

14. The issue of the large population of Muslim people in India and the formation of Pakistan is another very important dimension of Gandhi's life.

bhakti there can be no deliverance. Only he, therefore, wins deliverance who is devoted to duty and fills his heart with the love of God; he alone wins deliverance who never thinks about it."[15]

- Implied in the meaning of *bhakti* is *moksha*, salvation understood as deliverance from *samsara*, the cycle of birth and death. It is a fundamental goal of the deeply spiritual Hindu.
- Also suggested in the concepts of *bhakti* and *moksha* is the notion of *atman*, understood as the universal self that underlies individual personality. He understood *atman* as the heart of his spiritual goals.

Gandhi's spiritual journey was guided by these principles. Emerging from this spiritual quest were the values and goals of his life. I'll just mention four concepts:

- There was *satya*, best translated as "truth." He writes: "The word *satya* is derived from *sat*, which means that which is. Nothing exists in reality except Truth. That is why *sat* or *satya* is the right name for God. In fact it is more correct to say that Truth is God than to say that God is truth."[16] Above all, Gandhi sought to understand the truth and be guided by it.[17]
- Derived from his convictions about truth is a way of describing his leadership in leading India to independence. The way of leading this endeavor was called *satyagraha*, often translated as "truth-force." Gandhi deeply believed that the truth would prevail in seeking India's independence and the overthrow of colonialism.
- The means of achieving this goal must be *ahimsa*, best translated as "nonviolence." Led by truth, nonviolence, and the respect for all of life, one engages in the goal of achieving justice by using the practice of nonviolent resistance, resisting falsehood and what is fundamentally harmful to all of life. From this commitment of Gandhi's came the further development of the concept of civil disobedience, central to the work of Martin Luther King Jr.
- Later, as part of the path to freedom, Gandhi would argue for the dismantling of *varna*, best understood as the class system and the four

---

15. Brown, *Mahatma Gandhi*, 6.
16. Brown, *Mahatma Gandhi*, 44.
17. Such a commitment is rare among American politicians.

divisions of Hindu society, privileged classes supported in many ways by the non-caste or outcaste population. He writes: "I believe that every man [person] is born in this world with certain natural tendencies. Every person is born with certain limitations, which he cannot overcome. From careful observation of these limitations the law of *varna* was deduced. It established certain spheres of action of certain people with certain tendencies . . . This great law has been degraded and has fallen into disrepute."[18] He goes to say that this distorted understanding and practice must be changed, enabling the freedom of all people to find and follow their understanding of a true way in life.

It would be hard to overstate the positive influence that Gandhi, the great soul, had on the country of India, the region of South Asia, and indeed most of the world. He demonstrated in a remarkable way how his understanding of Transcendence, rooted in Hinduism, could be and was instrumental in transforming India and providing positive guidance to many other countries of the world.

---

18. Brown, *Mahatma Gandhi*, 101.

7

Committed Spirituality
The Ways of Obedience and Faithfulness

WE CONTINUE OUR THEME of exploring the ways that those of us who live in the modern and postmodern world have sought to understand transcendence, believing or perhaps just hoping that it may point us to the true Divine Transcendence.[1] We noted that across time this quest has had and continues to have three broad metaphorical directions. Many have studied the religious setting in which they find themselves, looking *outward* to the world around them, to nature and to their unique history as a way of finding an undergirding principle or Source that would bring guidance. These seekers believed that this outlook would help understand how they should live in order to find meaning in life, ways to flourish, and ways to create a just and humane social order. Others, certainly aware of the natural and social world in which they live and their history, have focused more on looking *inward* through contemplation and meditation to find guidance for life. We also suggested another direction in our quest, looking *upward* to a personal God, made known by a great founder and a trustworthy record with an attempt to live faithfully and obediently to the will and way of the Divine One.

---

1. Many of us also think that it might not point us anywhere except to scientific inquiry and a continuing desire to learn and know.

Committed Spirituality

We have already, although briefly, introduced the perspectives (ways of seeing) that attempt to bring a Christian way of understanding Transcendence into the present world. Christians, as have most of the world's religions, have partially used all three outlooks—outward, inward, and upward—in the hope that it will be a more relevant reflection of the divine will and way. They have drawn upon these ways of seeing across history and now, as have nearly all religions, have searched for ways of understanding that make their faith relevant and credible in the modern and postmodern world. They have asked how it might be possible to discern the divine will and way of God and then live faithfully and obediently to it in the tumultuous twenty-first century. The answer is book-length and lifelong and we can only suggest patterns rather than full descriptions that seek to have integrity with the dramatic shifts in a contemporary worldview.

We have already looked briefly at one attempt to bring Christian understanding into the contemporary world, one that attempts to integrate or at least lives in harmony with the scientific understanding of the world. We mentioned the theological perspective called *creation spirituality*, thoughtfully developed by Matthew Fox, which points to the goodness and blessing of creation. This outlook maintains that through historical inquiry, science, and, in particular, discerning the patterns of evolution we can find an authentic pattern, authored by divine Transcendence, which will guide us in our quest to find meaning, health, and inner contentment. It is a point of view that challenges the traditional Christian understanding of a cosmic fall and original sin and offers Christians a way to integrate their faith with a more contemporary worldview. In this view, the cosmic fall in the garden is a mythical and poetic story of the early development of humankind, and *original sin* is but another name for evolution. We then turned to the writing of Pierre Teilhard de Chardin, in which he articulates a way to integrate science and Christian faith. He views them as complementary and suggestive of a divine presence and pattern for life. He too leans against the more negative view of human nature inherent in the doctrine of original sin and the cosmic fall of humankind and, using a scientific understanding of evolution, points to a positive future for the world, an Omega Point when God will bring creation to its full realization.

I would now like to focus our attention on the ways that Judaism and Islam have also sought to make their beliefs and practices both credible and relevant to the contemporary world. As we do, I want to underline once again that there is generally some tension and criticism present in this endeavor. There are those on the conservative side of a religious tradition that want to preserve the purity of what they consider to be the original revelation, coming in the form of a person such as Moses, Jesus, or Muhammad, then contained in and continued through inspired writing as in the case of the Bible and the Quran, and then followed by a trustworthy tradition that existed and was maintained in the religious community. There is the deep fear that a new direction will distort these fundamentals of the true faith. On the other hand, there are many in the faith tradition that may want to shift and reframe the beliefs and practices in a way that makes them more acceptable, credible, and germane to modern people. Generally, the feelings are intense as one gets to the outer edges of both conservative and more progressive perspectives, with the conservative side often tending toward judgmental, exclusive, and tribal behavior. On the progressive side, there is a tendency to discount the extreme conservative position as almost superstitious and then, as the liberal edge describes their views, they may actually move beyond foundational beliefs. As a general rule, there are those that have taken the middle way, avoiding the extremes and seeking integration, and they have tended to prevail, sensing an element of truth on both sides and bringing these elements to the place of belief and action. Buddhism, for example, in its own particular way, elevates the middle way between extreme asceticism and fixed beliefs and a good measure of freedom of belief and practice as the best spiritual pathway.

MODERN JUDAISM

Modern Judaism, both its conservative and liberal patterns, has found a way to cope with and even thrive in the contemporary world. One remarkable way it has found to deal with and accommodate these patterns of conservative and liberal beliefs and practices is to recognize and accept that the Jewish people are quite diverse, coming from very different backgrounds and histories. Many Jews have said, "Let's live with it." Although at times there is conflict and tension, they have generally accepted and realistically managed their diversity.

There are groupings of Jews with different histories, nationalities, cultures, and languages. In some measure these differences reflect that they have been discriminated against and persecuted, and often they have had to seek safer locations. Their religious outlook, as it has been with most religions, reflects their history. Inevitably, they have had to form different branches or, to use a term more frequently found in the Christian church, different *denominations*. For example, a quick glance at contemporary Judaism would suggest that there are three major patterns with several subgroups:[2]

- There is Orthodox Judaism, a branch that considers all Jewish law and several religious practices and customs, such as even clothing from a particular era, as binding. Many of these beliefs and practices that emerged in a particular time and culture have become the expected norm. There is quite a strong Orthodox Jewish presence in Israel and the United States, and an element of it in other parts of the world.

- There is Conservative Judaism, a branch that believes in the obligation to obey Jewish law, and yet this law, the *Halakhah*, evolves according to new insights and knowledge. Modest change is acceptable, yet the Jewish identity is clearly preserved and reflected in their beliefs and practices.

- There is Reform Judaism, a movement that does not consider all Jewish law as binding and seeks to find thoughtful ways for Judaism to fit into the best expressions of religious thought and ethical standards present in modernity.

We might also mention that a large number of Jews would understand themselves as secular, respecting a long tradition that gives them their identity but not by accepting the theological outlook or engaging in the religious practices of Judaism.

In addition, there are movements within Judaism that have developed in reference to their particular historical circumstances. For example, the Ashkenazi Jews had their origins in Central Europe and trace their ancestry to medieval Germany. There were major migrations of these Jews to Poland and Russia between the twelfth and sixteenth centuries. The Sephardim Jews descended from those people who lived in Spain. These two major branches have a good measure of understanding and empathy for the other, acknowledging their different histories. Both of these groups, many of which had immigrated to Germany, experienced what is perhaps the most tragic event in their history, the Holocaust, during the Hitler regime. This horrendous event profoundly shaped modern Judaism. There is a strong

---

2. See Lawrence J. Epstein's book *The Basic Beliefs of Judaism: A Twenty-First-Century Guide to a Timeless Tradition*, for a brief account of the beliefs, practices, and the historical development of Judaism.

Section Two: The Modern Quest to Understand and Connect with Transcendence

sense among them that they must deal directly with the realities of almost universal discrimination against Jewish people.

A brief historical sketch of the Jewish people and their religion reveals a second factor, in addition to the acceptance of their diversity, that has enabled Judaism to sustain its vitality in the contemporary world. It is the way they have been willing to accent and modify their belief system in reference to the Enlightenment, the rise of science, the emergence of capitalist economies, and other historical developments that fed into the formation of the modern world. Even with the tension that this modification has caused, there is still a set of core beliefs and practices that is present worldwide in the Jewish family. They have found good ways to articulate their faith and bring their foundational beliefs and practices into the modern world. As we illustrate this point, it is important to mention again that not all Jews practice the religion of Judaism, and not all those who follow the teaching of Judaism are Jewish. There are secular Jews, and there are converts to Judaism from non-Jewish backgrounds.

There are dimensions of their beliefs and practices, whether they live in Tel Aviv or New York, that have held them together as a distinctive people and enabled them to enter fully into the contemporary world. They have done so without denying their history. Perhaps as much as any group of people in the world, they have honored and respected their common history. It gives them the outline of their identity. The biblical stories of their different locations, their difficult and challenging circumstances, and the presence of comforting wisdom found in collections such as the Psalms and Proverbs are integral to their beliefs and practices and speak to the contemporary world. Judaism has a clear message for all people, and there is a great deal of history and literature from which to draw.

Judaism is certainly one of the oldest continuing worldwide religions. It had its beginnings as far back as about 2000 BCE in the region of ancient Babylonia. Abraham, thought to be the founder and father of Judaism, came from Ur of the Chaldeans in Babylonia.[3] His story and his travels west to Canaan are recorded in the Bible, and with careful historical study his life and beliefs have provided guidance and insight into the origins of Judaism, the Jewish people, and their way of life and beliefs.[4] It is a fascinating story of tribes, travels, and the ebb and flow of empires. In time, as the story

---

3. Martin Goodman, Professor of Jewish Studies at the University of Oxford, has written an excellent book entitled *A History of Judaism*, and I am guided by it.

4. It also informs Christianity and Islam.

unfolds, we are introduced to Moses in Egypt, the exodus, the empire under King David, the voices of the prophets, the formation of the temple and synagogues, the emergence of the *Torah* as the foundational teaching, and the development of rabbinic law and practice. In time, these people, living on the eastern edge of the Mediterranean Sea, became a nation and were assimilated into the Greco-Roman world.

In the time of Roman occupation, their religion and its leadership evolved and adjusted to this occupation. For example, there were various groups with different views and functions. There were the religious and political leaders from the Pharisees and Sadducees, and a smaller group called the Essenes, who left the geographical center of Judaism in Jerusalem and moved close to the Dead Sea for the sake of purity. Another group, called the Zealots, led the resistance to Roman occupation. In time, Jesus appeared on the scene and the apostle Paul promoted the development of a new branch of Judaism that would later be called Christianity. Mainline Judaism evolved with an emphasis on purity in its legal codes, the practice of the Sabbath, and wide range of beliefs and practices that included vows and visions of the future, one of which was the notion of the coming of a messiah. These people, a modest population, somehow managed to survive under the Roman occupation and continued to develop their religious beliefs and practices. Their religion, Judaism, became a religion that was led and guided by those with the vocation of rabbi, who gave leadership to the temple, its beliefs, and the continuing socialization of religious practice. As history unfolded, they had to deal with an indigenous population, foreign invasions, and a range of complex issues. There are clear lessons in this history for the present world.

Another component of their beliefs and practices that has enabled the Jewish people and the religion of Judaism to survive, and in some cases even thrive, in the modern world is the way they have sustained their foundational beliefs and articulated them in a manner that recognizes and accommodates them to a contemporary worldview, yet preserves the heart of their basic beliefs and practices. For example, they continue to believe in and worship a personal God, whom they believe has been active in their history. But their articulation of this belief has been integrated into contemporary thought by many fine Jewish scholars and teachers. For example, Martin Buber's classic work *I and Thou* spoke profoundly to a whole generation of people grappling with all of the concerns of existential thought. It was deeply moving for me as I came of age in the 1960s and 1970s. Abraham

Section Two: The Modern Quest to Understand and Connect with Transcendence

Heschel's books *God in Search of Man* and *Man Is Not Alone* underlined the universality of Judaism and spoke to lost souls of all kinds unable to find their way in the modern world.

In addition, Judaism has continued to provide a strong sense of values and ethical norms, guiding not only Jewish people, but many who search for meaning and purpose in a time without a commonly accepted sense of what is right and what is wrong. Judaism has a strong belief that we do not live in a random world, but one created by God, and that as one lives in this world there is divine guidance and a system of accountability. Both the *Torah* (Law) and the *Talmud* (how this ethical and social system has developed and been interpreted) formed across the dramatic history of the Jewish people and have provided the ethical norms and illustrative stories to guide the people. We have all read and understood that there are Ten Commandments. And in many parts of the world, there is the regional synagogue with the local rabbi's responsibility to teach these grand stories and their lessons.

I want to mention an additional way that modern Judaism has integrated into and serves the contemporary world, and that is its emphasis on compassion and justice and its vision to remake the world. A fundamental teaching of Judaism is that its followers are called to join with God in creating a more just and humane world.

This emphasis on teaching the followers of Judaism to serve the world by being compassionate and seeking justice needs some expansion. The story of this accommodation by Judaism to the contemporary world is a book-length subject and beyond our scope, but a few examples of how they have engaged in creating a more just and humane world will give us some understanding of how Judaism made its way into modernity.

One example that stands out and that has been demanding in scope and controversial in implementation is the formation of the nation of Israel. The formation of the nation on the eastern edge of the Mediterranean Sea was viewed by them as divinely inspired because it was a region in which most of Jewish history occurred. It became a safe haven for Jews around the world, and particularly those Jews who had been persecuted in the Holocaust. Most Jews understood the formation of the nation of Israel as an act of compassion and justice, although there were many who saw it as an act of aggression. This endeavor was largely supported by world powers such as the United States and many of the European countries. Yet there was strong resistance by many of the Arab countries, and a great many native Palestinians were forced to leave their homes. This has been one of the most difficult problems to solve in the region and the world; there is little doubt that there are many who lived in the region of Palestine who were and are victims of social injustice created by what has become an essentially Jewish country.

The Jewish people, regardless of location, have always valued education, a key component of how the Jewish people and followers of Judaism have fully entered into the contemporary world. Many Jewish people have become intellectual leaders of the world, including such people as Albert Einstein. They have made extraordinary contributions to global understanding. Except in a few rare cases, the integration of Jewish faith with modern knowledge has not been difficult; indeed it has been profoundly appreciated and honored. Deep divisions, based on worldviews rooted in the ancient world over against those undergirded by contemporary worldviews, do exist, as for example among Orthodox Jews. But for the most part these differences of outlook have not been difficult to overcome in Judaism. Recently deceased Rabbi Lord Jonathan Sachs is a prime example. He has been recognized as an international religious leader, active in ecumenical and interfaith conversation and collaboration, chaplain to the Queen of England, philosopher and theologian, and award-winning author. He was a respected as moral voice. His recent book, *Morality: Restoring the Common Good in Divided Times*, has been widely read, respected well beyond the Jewish community in the United Kingdom, and has met a deep need for describing moral convictions that are universal.

I will provide one more example of the way that Judaism has emerged as a religion and spiritual pathway that has managed to become an attractive contemporary option for people in the modern world. A perennial problem for all of the world's great religions, guided by historical charismatic leaders and ancient documents, is the challenge of treating all people fairly. Almost inevitably, there are those who are insiders who do not trust or even accept those who, because of their beliefs and practices, do not fit traditional patterns, cultural norms, and ethical expectations. Women and men, those with different status because of wealth or education, those from different cultures with different languages and customs, those with darker or lighter skin, have generally been treated with honor, respect, and justice by the worldwide Jewish community. To be sure, some groups of Jewish people, deeply committed and loyal to their smaller group, have harshly judged and mistreated those who are different, as for example native Palestinians and even other Jews from a different branch of Judaism. But this behavior goes against the finest teaching within Judaism. There are honest accounts in the Bible of those who have been prejudiced against those who are *other* due to different backgrounds, cultural norms, languages, and behavior. But the finest ethical guidance of the Hebrew Bible could not be clearer; we are to honor those who are different, treating them with respect and ensuring that they will be treated fairly and justly. The great prophets nudged this point even further and said that compassion for the needy and the foreigner is fundamental. Faithful Jews are called to make the world better.

One way that this great teaching in the Hebrew Bible has been applied in recent times is the ways in which Jewish women are respected and not bound by traditional roles. There is still a division of labor within some Jewish families and differences in family structure and roles among the branches of Judaism. Often the women in the family do care for the children in special ways and provide a home setting that is comfortable and pleasant. But for the majority of Jewish people these traditional roles no longer carry a religious sanction. Jewish women are encouraged to pursue their education and chose their careers on the basis of interests and ability. They could just as easily be and have been the Prime Minister of Israel (Golda Meir), members of the US Supreme Court (Ruth Bader Ginsburg), or the president of a leading university or international company. I have been informed and inspired by many women rabbis.

Tensions continue to exist in Judaism between those with a modern outlook and those who seek to maintain beliefs and practices of a bygone era, and perhaps this is generally the case in most religious settings. But it is more often the case that leaders of Judaism have found in their faith great resources for navigating the treacherous waters of contemporary life. Their history and beliefs are filled with traces of transcendence that can inform and guide us.

ISLAM

Islam is a term coming from Arabic, which literally means submission or surrender to the will of God. A Muslim is one who is committed to this submission to God and practices the religion of Islam. Islam shares this foundational belief with its Abrahamic monotheistic cousins, Judaism and Christianity. There are other beliefs and practices that Islam shares with them as well, although each of the religions has a distinctive expression of

Committed Spirituality

them. Using our directional metaphors, it is a religion whose followers look *upward*, believing that a personal God has communicated the divine will and way through a person, Muhammad, and a book, the Quran. It is a religion serving over 1.5 billion people, second only to Christianity in size, with its followers located in South Asia (India, Pakistan, and Bangladesh), North Africa, the Middle East, Iran, Turkey, Indonesia, Malaysia, China, and an increasing number in Western Europe and North and South America.

Islam has its origins in the region now called Saudi Arabia, in the city of Mecca in about 570 CE. In this city, Muhammad was born, and because of the early death of his parents he was raised by his grandfather, and later by his uncle, who was widely respected leader in the world of trade and known for his integrity. At the age of twenty-five, Muhammad married an older woman, Khadija, who was wise and kind, and they had four daughters. She guided and supported her younger husband and accepted the cultural norm of allowing for other wives, often taken in as a philanthropic act. As he matured, he joined his uncle in the family business and was successful, although in time he began his quest to find religious answers to life's most troubling questions. He made regular retreats to a nearby cave to meditate and pray, and it was in this setting that he received the religious wisdom and insight that was to become the heart of the Quran. The central message of these revelations, thought to have come from the archangel Gabriel, was that God (Allah) is full of mercy and compassion. As these insights were shared and written, they became known as the Quran, or the Recitation, using the term *recitation* because the Quran was generally read out loud, in part to underline the message and in part because many of the listeners could not read. Some of his insight and reflections had connections to the history and beliefs of Judaism and Christianity, although with a distinctive message germane to the region, its culture, and language.[5]

This new movement grew dramatically and spread to the surrounding region, and soon there was a community of believers called the *ummah*. A constitution was developed as the movement became centered in the city of Medina, and it contained several guiding principles of the new religion, including a measure of religious freedom, the security of women, and guidance

---

5. An excellent introduction to Islam is John L. Esposito's *Islam*. There is an excellent coffee-table volume by Seddon and Bokhar entitled *The Illustrated Encyclopedia of Islam*, with wonderful pictures and a clear explanation of the many sides of Islam.

for peace among the warring tribes.⁶ Within a few short years, there was agreement on the basic beliefs and practices of Islam: The beliefs are:

1. the affirmation of the unity and oneness of God;
2. that God communicates to the creation;
3. that God is the creator of all that is;
4. that there will be a final judgment, based on the divine decrees and predestination;
5. that there will be a community of believers, the *ummah*, for the guiding the people.

From these foundational beliefs, there follows the Five Pillars of practice:

1. the *Shahadah*, professing that there is no god but God and that Muhammad is the messenger of God;
2. the *Salat*, five daily prayers said facing the *Ka'bah*, the sacred cubicle in Mecca;
3. the *Sakat*, obligatory annual almsgiving;
4. *Ramadan*, the month of fasting;
5. the *Hajj*, the pilgrimage to the sacred places of Islam that all Muslims, as they are able, must make.

On occasion, another practice is mentioned called *jihad*, a profound effort or endeavor to sustain the spiritual goals and straight path of Islam.

It wasn't long after the founding of Islam that a vast region began to be shaped by this new religion. The presence of the *ummah*, the community of believers, soon altered traditional patterns of the social order. The Muslim sense of community was very strong and the teaching of Islam soon influenced the shape of the society. There was the weekly gathering in what was to become the mosque, with regular ritual practice and the teaching that all of life should be based on the teachings of Islam. The word *din*, often translated as "religion," taught that Muslims are to respond obediently to God and follow the "straight path." Soon, there was the presence of *shariah* or law that described the sum of duties for all Muslim people.⁷

---

6. Allen, and Shawkat, eds., *Islam: A Short Guide to the Faith*, 6–8.

7. See the account in my book *Exploring the Spirituality of the World Religions*, 190–203. As time passed, there were different understandings of the law.

Committed Spirituality

Following the death of Muhammad, with the religious center in Medina, new leaders were selected called *caliphs*, who ruled over the new territories that were essentially conquered and now Muslim in character. These new regions were managed in way that ensured the practice of Islam. A common pattern of laws and rules, based on the new literature, the Quran, came into existence and had influence over both the social systems and personal behavior. Even the cities formed earlier with different patterns of governance and ways of life were modified to fit the requirements of *sharia* (law).

Early in the life of Islam, there were the challenges of finding the leadership that would take the place of Muhammad. Divisions developed, although initially Abu Bakr, the father-in-law of Muhammad, provided the primary leadership and was called the *caliph*. Following his death, there were a number of movements that sought to be the guiding center of the new religion. The two largest groups were the Shia and the Sunni, ones that continue to give leadership, yet they have differences that have lasted into the present. The Shia (meaning followers) maintained that the person chosen to lead should come from the descendants of Muhammad. Those holding this position reasoned that the caliph, as a descendant of Muhammad, would be endowed with divinely inspired leadership abilities, have the ability to correctly interpret the Quran, and have the capacity to guide the faithful followers.[8] Another group, the Sunnis, maintained that the selection of the caliph, the leader and of the religion and the country, should be selected on the basis of natural abilities, and this group soon emerged as having the majority of support. A number of other smaller groups also developed, believing they could lead and provide the most authentic form of Islam. Many of these divisions continue into the present and reflect their unique history, culture, customs, language, and the settings in which they developed. Islam, not unlike Christianity, became quite diverse, yet did not lose its center.[9]

It is this diversity, adjusting the core beliefs and practices to the particular environments, that has enabled the dramatic spread of Islam. In some cases, the presence of Islam genuinely altered the customs and culture of the new setting, while in other settings Islam was integrated into the character of the new setting. It is this flexible feature of Islam that is one factor that has contributed to Islam's ability to meet the religious needs of people

---

8. The title of *imam* is generally used for leaders of local congregations, not unlike the terms *minister*, *pastor*, and *priest*.

9. Aslan, Reza, *Not god But God*.

Section Two: The Modern Quest to Understand and Connect with Transcendence

from difficult cultures. The dramatic expansion has not been without the continuation of conflict, much of which other parts of the world have observed, particularly in the part of Islam that has a radical dimension. Most dramatic has been the conflict between Shia and Sunni, with each having a political as well as a religious base. Indeed, many countries identify themselves as being loyal to either the Shia or Sunni branches of Islam, and the different interpretations of Islam have even contributed to conflict between these countries.

The movement of Islam into the modern world has been challenging, yet it has done so in a remarkable way. I want to suggest five interwoven ways that have made the religious outlook of Islam more acceptable in the contemporary context, or at least widely accepted and honored by those who live in Muslim countries where the beliefs and practices of Islam shape the culture of the country.

The first of these characteristics of Islam that has contributed to its acceptance and growth in the contemporary world is that it clearly invites the seeker into a cohesive and comprehensive way of life.[10] Islam asks for and receives a total commitment and then provides guidance on what to believe (creed) and how to live (code of ethics). It invites the believer to place their loyalty and pattern of life into a religion that promises to guide its followers in a pattern of worship and practice that is both clear and direct. Islam's community then comes along side of the faithful follower with support that will undergird their beliefs and empower them to practice its teachings. Followers have a sense of belonging to a community that understands Allah's will and way and provides a clear pattern for the individual to be on the straight path.

Secondly, as a slight expansion of the first characteristic, is that the "straight path" is brief, clearly defined, and understandable. There are the Five Pillars of practice that outline the spiritual pathway of a Muslim. There is one God to whom one prays, a clear setting and guidance on how and when to offer these prayers, a way to help those in need through the expected alms giving, a rhythm of worship and celebration through the year with special times and seasons such as Ramadan, and the goal to make the sacred journey to Mecca called the *Hajj*. This frame of reference provides the Muslim with a comprehensive worldview, one that makes sense out of confusing world and offers a pattern of life that is straightforward and appealing.

---

10. See my book *The Spirituality of the World Religions*, 200–201.

Committed Spirituality

It is not only that the steps in the spiritual journey are clear and possible to take, but it is also the case that the simple belief system is understandable, even to those without a formal education. There is simple and clear set of beliefs that flow together and can be endorsed as a consistent system of thought. This pattern of beliefs is anchored by the understanding of the nature of Allah.

> In the name of Allah, most gracious, most merciful
> All praise is due to Allah, the Lord of the Worlds
> The Most Gracious, the most Merciful,
> You alone we worship
> And from you along we seek help
> Guide us on the right path,
> the path of those on whom you have bestowed grace,
> not of those with whom you have been displeased,
> nor those who have gone astray. (Surah 1:1–7)

A fourth dimension of Islam that has a good measure of appeal to modern people is that one inherits a supportive community and the sense of belonging to that most important community in the world. It is the community of God, of Allah. It is one in which there is clear guidance on both belief and practice. One becomes a member of a worldwide family of faith, one that has the practice of benevolence for those in great need. It is no secret that much of our experience in the contemporary world, especially in the more secular settings in which we live, often leads to insecurity and anxiety, and the feelings of being lost and lonely. We are rushed, meeting the demands of work, struggling to have sufficient income to adequately meet family needs, and often feeling isolated from others. It is a competitive world where friendship is secondary to performance and level of income. It is also a diverse world, one in which even in our local neighborhood we may not know the name of the person who lives next door. Our needs for friendship and mutual support are often met in the church, synagogue, or mosque.

One additional dimension of Islam, although one that is far from being perfect and in which there is still more that needs to be done, is that it has tried to integrate its religious beliefs with the prevailing contemporary worldview. This integrative work is being done on several levels: in the world of scientific understanding, in the world of global infrastructure, in the world of politics and the complex arena of international relations, in the world of ethics, in the world of benevolence, and in the world that provides a pathway to fulfillment, happiness, and a full measure of inner peace. It is beyond our scope to unpack all of these modern developments within the Islamic world. But I do want to say a word about this last domain, the domain of health and contentment. Islam, as do most religious traditions, speaks to the harsh reality that inner peace for most of us is elusive and hard to attain. There is one branch of Islam that has put an emphasis on finding a center and pattern of life that leads to health and inner contentment, Sufism.

Sufism may best be understood as Islamic mysticism with its teaching about how to cultivate a deep and profound spirituality.[11] The goal of the Sufi is to take an inner journey that empowers them to achieve closeness to God. Sufis are keenly aware that other values, such as the quest for money and possessions, for power and fame, and for ego gratification, can lead the Sufi pilgrim astray. These values must be given up for the primary value of having a pure soul. Sufi teachers point to the fact the Prophet, Muhammad, took the same journey. In fact, he too had to resist the temptation of following the norms of his culture. He was surrounded and tempted by those with wealth and power, those who sought fame, and those driven by the need to gratify their ego. Yet he was victorious over these temptations, and Sufis seek to follow his example.

The word *Sufism* partially comes from an Arabic term meaning "wearing woolen garments," a symbol of wealth, and the early Sufi followers would tear up their woolen clothes as a as a symbol of giving up wealth and their dedication to purify their soul. Another possible meaning of the term is that it was a reference to "those on the platform," that is, those who sought power and fame. The Sufi movement counseled against this desire to be "on the platform" in that it meant that being the center of attention and ego gratification were the most important values. But what is most important is the development of the soul; this must be the primary value in life.

Many Sufis turned toward extreme asceticism, although it was certainly possible to be active in community life and then model the values of dedication to the spiritual life. In time, this movement was organized and set guiding principles, established orders not unlike Roman Catholic orders, and suggested that those who sought a deep and profound spirituality should have a spiritual director.

One of the best-known Sufis, a person whose wisdom is valued today in many parts of the world, is Jalal-Ud-Din Rumi (1207–1273). He wrote the spiritual classic *Mathnawi*, a work that has been translated into many

---

11. Seddon and Bokhar, *Illustrated Encyclopedia of Islam*, 240–47.

languages and has inspired those from many religious traditions. For example, he writes: "It is God's privilege to test us anytime He fancies so that He can reveal what lies deep in our hearts."[12] This brief saying is but one example of hundreds of wise observations and aphorisms about life.

It is significant that another classic teacher of the Sufi was a woman, Rabiah Al-Adawiyyah (717–801), who is described as the first Sufi woman and a model of sainthood. She lived in the region of the world that is now known as Iraq and had a profound influence on the spiritual practices of Muslims in that region. It was a setting in which she was able both to model a profoundly spiritual life and to write about the pathway of Sufi spirituality. She is perhaps best known for her explanation of the concept of *sidq*, or the need to be sincere (authentic) in one's faith and spiritual journey. She was especially hard on those that took pride in their ascetic lifestyle and emphasized that it is what is inside of the believer, true dedication as opposed to external symbols, that is important. She wrote about her own spirituality: "I ask God's forgiveness for my lack of truthfulness and sincerity in saying 'I ask God's forgiveness.'"[13]

I have a close friend and colleague who is a Sufi Muslim imam who serves as pastor of an interreligious congregation in Seattle. It has been my privilege to partner with him in ministries of teaching, writing, and interreligious and ecumenical understanding and collaboration. He is a model of what it means to be a dedicated Sufi Muslim and one who has a deep spiritual pathway. He is invited to speak across the United States along with a rabbi and Protestant pastor on interfaith understanding. They are called "The Interfaith Amigos" and they have provided guidance to many groups on how to understand and appreciate those with a different religious orientation. My friend teaches me on a regular basis and helps many others understand how Islam may easily be made relevant and credible in the contemporary world. His Sufi orientation has great appeal to those who are seeking a deep spirituality, and it addresses a profound quest in many parts of the world to find meaning and to flourish. He contributes to helping others see a side of Islam that enters fully into the contemporary world.

We turn now to several other expressions of Transcendence that find and articulate traces of the Divine in the universal values of truth, authenticity, love, compassion, and justice.

---

12. Mafi, trans., *Rumi Day by Day*, 42.
13. Seddon and Bokhar, *Illustrated Encyclopedia of Islam*, 247.

Section Three

The Current Practices of Spirituality

A peaceful heart gives birth to love. When love meets suffering, it turns to compassion. When love meets happiness, it turns to joy.[1]

—JACK KORNFIELD

---

1. Kornfield, *Wise Heart*, 387.

8

Compassionate Spirituality
The Ways of Implementing Universal Values

INHERENT TRANSCENDENCE

WE ARE NOW READY to explore the ways that the world into which we are born reflects design and structure (transcendence), patterns that were experienced and honored, although not understood scientifically, by those living in the premodern era. These patterns are now understood and explained by modern scholarship, primarily in the natural sciences, but also in the social sciences and humanities. The sciences have developed a massive system of describing the natural world, outlining even for non-scientists the ways that the universe has an order and way of functioning. Added to these scientific discoveries have been the ways humans have learned to understand, admire, and live in heartfelt ways in their natural and inherent home, mother earth. My science-oriented friends explain to me how the beautiful mountains of central Oregon were formed, evolved, and are gradually changing, and my literary and poetic friends share my love of their magnificent grandeur. We view them with awe and wonder as we hike and bike. This built-in transcendence for many in our secular world is all that is needed to manage and appreciate life. We are able to flourish if we have the capacity to see and understand. We catch on, collaborate, appreciate, and

Section Three: The Current Practices of Spirituality

cooperate with this transcendence. Ways have been found to affirm and utilize these universal values.

We have spoken about the human belief that there is a transcendent power beyond nature and history, one that created this beautiful landscape and has been active in evolution and human history. We have spoken about the ways that humans have understood this Source and Presence and described the ways of comprehending it and connecting with this Transcendence in many ways, ways that we have summarized in three directional metaphors. There are those who look *outward* to nature and history and sense a divine purpose; there are those who turn *inward* and believe they get in touch with this deeper reality; and then there are those who look *upward* to divine transcendence, see it as the revelation of a divine reality that is beyond nature and history and has created and continues to shape them. In this chapter, we want to focus on those who are less inclined to look for a divine presence and power beyond nature and history and seek to find natural patterns and rhythms that point to more universal values in the world they inhabit to guide them. Our question is whether these transcendent realities within the earth and universe that we inhabit will help us understand and find guidance for meaning and purpose in life. No less a scientist than Edward O. Wilson writes: "We were created not by a supernatural intelligence but by chance and necessity as one species out of millions of species in Earth's biosphere."[1] He adds that not relying on belief in a supernatural order and prescriptive behavior sets us free and invites us to collaborate with nature in order to have a full life and to create a more just and humane social order. Richard Dawkins, a British scientist, is even more direct in rejecting a belief in divine Transcendence. For example, he writes: "The God of the Old Testament is arguably the most unpleasant character in all of fiction: jealous and proud of it; petty, unjust, unforgiving control-freak; vindictive, bloodthirsty ethnic cleanser; a misogynistic, homophopic, racist, infanticidal, genocidal, filicidal, pestilential, megalomaniacal, sadomasochistic, capriciously malevolent bully."[2] This kind of god nobody needs, although if I were in conversation with him, I would say that there are better and more accurate and engaging ways to understand the Hebrew Bible and Transcendence. Yet he makes a good case, and I even learned a few new words, although his argument could be more nuanced and balanced.

---

1. Wilson, *Meaning of Human Existence*, 173.
2. Dawkins, *God Delusion*, 31.

Both of these scientists with many colleagues would argue that there is really no evidence to suggest a divine Presence beyond or active in the structures of the universe or the course of human history. They would also maintain that there is transcendence brilliantly described by modern science, not only in the natural sciences, but in the descriptive human sciences as well. We are able to discover how to live maturely and responsibly (*The Meaning of Human Existence* is one of Edward O. Wilson's book titles) in our world as we piece together its patterns and rhythms. In fact, to discern this built-in infrastructure provides us with a much more credible and less superstitious pattern of life. I partially agree with this point of view, but sometimes wonder why they do not acknowledge and appreciate those positions that ascribe a divine Presence in nature and history, yet also afirm a scientific understanding of the world and attempt to integrate the two views. For example, we have mentioned the theological outlook of creation spirituality, which underlines the need to keep a clear and scientific eye on nature, suggests patterns of contemplative spirituality based on human development, and carefully studies the flow of history while working diligently for a more just and peaceful world.

I have been informed in my reading across many years of studying these more secular points of view that there is a clear affirmation of deep universal values that point the way to healthy, compassionate, and responsible living. I have also had the privilege of working with government agencies and private foundations, clearly secular in their orientation, yet engaged in the pursuit of improving education, addressing world hunger, providing health resources, creating employment opportunities, building more just social structures, and seeking peaceful solutions to deep conflicts and reducing violence. In these endeavors, there have been clear goals rooted in transcendent values that undergird a more empathic infrastructure. It is these transcendent values that have a nearly universal acceptance that we now want to understand and describe. And we will ask along the way if there is at least a hint of piggybacking on what we have called *transcendent values* that suggest a trace of the Divine in them.

THE EARTH CHARTER

As a way of articulating these values, I would like to draw upon the goals of UNESCO in their document entitled *The Earth Charter*, published in

Section Three: The Current Practices of Spirituality

Paris in March of 2000.[3] It is admittedly a bit dated and was prepared as a guide to United Nations policy and practice at the start of the new millennium. It represents the values of people from many different countries, and there is little or no reference to the ground of being or the Divine, and yet a clear and conscious effort to respect all people and indeed all of life, regardless of religious orientation or the lack of it. It suggests universal and transcendent values that guide people from many different countries and walks of life and is a response to a troubled world with problems that are now more serious and dangerous than they were just over two decades ago. We will attempt to make it current and a response to our particular time with an awareness of COVID-19 and the many challenges of our time and condition of our world. The charter has four universal goals:

1. creating an earth community of care and respect,
2. creating an earth environment with ecological integrity,
3. creating a global culture of social and economic justice,
4. creating a global context of democracy, nonviolence, and peace.

I want briefly to describe the most pressing problems facing the world at the turn of the century, problems that suggested the four universal goals. I then take each one of these goals, update and add to it, and see in what ways it may point to an inherent transcendence in the world we inhabit and suggest values that the whole human family can affirm. Wikipedia lists the global catastrophic risks that were present at the turn of the century, a list that needs only a little editing to be for the 2020s. The nine risks listed are:[4]

1. declining mental health,
2. increased climate change,
3. the role of artificial general intelligence,
4. biotechnology risks,
5. ecological collapse,
6. the place of molecular nanotechnology,
7. the threat of nuclear holocaust,

---

3. I did call attention to the *Earth Charter* in an earlier book, *Lovescapes: Mapping the Geography of Love*, 254.
4. https://en.wikipedia.org/wiki/List-of-global-issues.

Compassionate Spirituality

8. the challenges of overpopulation,

9. a global pandemic (sure enough, it came).

In the past two decades, these concerns have remained high risks and have only changed and been improved slightly by positive intervention. Many of these global risks, with only a little change in wording, would make a contemporary list as well, and it would not be too difficult to add a few risks that have emerged or developed since 2000. The accompanying material with this list includes concerns related to AIDS and indeed other health concerns, the use of atomic energy, the condition of children, excessive mining, little or no disarmament, lack of food, the challenge of governance, human rights, humanitarian assistance (immigration, refugees), people with disabilities, and limited water supply, all concerns in our time as well.

Other lists are present in the Wikipedia article. For example, there is the World Economic Forum list of challenges: food security, population growth, the future of work/unemployment, climate change, the financial crisis of 2007–2008, lack of gender equality, global trade and investment and regulatory frameworks, long-term investment strategy, and the future of healthcare. An additional list, focusing on the global environment, underlines the following concerns: overconsumption, overpopulation, biodiversity loss, deforestation, desertification, global warming/climate change, habitual destruction, Holocene (epoch) extinction, ocean acidification, ozone layer depletion, pollution, resource depletion, and urban sprawl. These lists suggest what was in the minds and hearts of those who prepared the four universal goals for the United Nations, and indirectly for many responsible governments and agencies.

Goal 1 underlines the need both to care for and respect our earth community. The implication of the language is that we are not there yet; that while there may be some level of care and respect in this large and diverse earth community, this level of care and respect must be increased in order to create a setting in which humankind, and indeed all life, can continue to exist and experience the fullness of life. The threatening problems appear to be almost overwhelming; they divide us and seriously threaten the good life and even life itself. Early in the decade, the world was reminded how far we have to go to care and respect mother earth and her family. On September 11, 2001, nineteen militants associated with the Islamic extremist group al Qaeda hijacked four airplanes and engaged in an attack on the United States. Two of the planes flew into the Twin Towers of the World Trade Center in New York City and a third and fourth plane attacked other targets. Nearly three thousand people were killed! It was just over one hundred minutes that changed American life and dramatically increased awareness of the threat of extremist groups in other parts of the world. Presidents Bush and Obama, in their respective terms of office and each in their own way, responded to this attack and what it represented in terms of the lack of care and respect for the earth community.

Following the presidency of Barack Obama, we passed into the Trump era, in which one part of the earth community, the United States, was deeply divided politically, so much so that it was nearly impossible to sustain a commitment to common goals and a sense of community, let alone care about global risks. The so-called big lie regarding who won the 2020 election, representing the larger issue of living in post-truth and soulless culture and the denial of reality, caused deep divisions in the United States. The attack on the Capitol put this division in headlines. Interwoven within the deep political divide has been the health concern of the COVID-19 pandemic. In addition to this health concern, there is the continuing challenge of environmental deterioration and global warming and a wide range of other concerns. We ask whether there are sufficient resources and will within governments, private initiatives, and the global infrastructure to solve these severe problems. Will humankind wake up and address the threats with care, wisdom, and knowledge?

The threats have been described and there are sincere and well-informed people calling for action. Yet in the quest for wealth, power, control, and narrow tribal and exclusive settings, a large portion of the population resists initiatives that address the threat of climate change and opposes initiatives of social justice that would distribute wealth more equitably and share political power in order to allow minorities to have a part in creating social structures that are fair and just. These attitudes present profound and severe limitations to change. These attitudes are apparent in developed countries, only partially disguised, and much more pronounced in developing countries, where hunger and violence are widespread; it is hard to think of the welfare of others if one is in desperate need. For many, there is a lack of resources to care for their own earth home. The irony is that our world has sufficient resources for all people. But conditions continue to exist that discriminate and even harm and abuse our common earth home and make it almost uninhabitable for many. Goal 1 of the UNESCO charter is right on target: create an earth community of care and respect.

We begin with goal 1, care and respect for our earth home, and the implication of the goal is that the earth in particular and the universe(s) is so vast and complicated, so amazing and beautiful, whose resources are so desperately needed, that it invites and almost commands our respect. We are humbled before its size, complexity, abundance, and beauty. One must be wearing blinders not to see its magnificence. Further, it is our home and the home of all sentient beings. We can tune in to earth's ways, cooperate, and collaborate with them, and integrate our efforts with these universal patterns. Our earth does have its own identity and functions largely within its own evolutionary development and structural design. As we understand its ways and resources, we must use our knowledge and abundance without abusing the source, build infrastructure that respects our earth home, and have a global decision-making system that honors the needs of all. The challenge to respect our earth home and function in these harmonious ways may appear to be almost overwhelming, but we must. The goal for us all to survive and even flourish demands that we respect our home, Mother Earth, while keeping an eye on the way our planetary home lives in a galactic neighborhood.

Respect for the earth is our starting point, but it needs to be translated into care, being wise in our use of the resources of our earth home and sustaining it with informed and positive interventions, and in many cases correcting our mistakes of the past. Care implies that we use the energy and resources of the earth in wise ways in order to sustain its value and continue to provide a setting for all those who live within its patterns and resources. There is clear evidence that its value has been threatened in the past and continues to be threatened in the present.

The second goal of the United Nations *Earth Charter* is to "create an earth environment with ecological integrity." It is almost redundant to list all of the global environmental concerns and challenges that we face. The range of threats are listed in a variety of publications, are addressed by many levels of government, clearly acknowledged as a threat to the world economy, and challenge most of us daily as we eat, work, and care for our families. At the risk of repetition, I want to once again call attention to climate change, global warming, and the threat to our environment. I call attention to these three dimensions of the challenge, interrelated as they are, but which call for slightly different strategies to address them. We look first at the way the goal is worded. There is the assumption that the environment in which we live can be improved; the direction is to create a better earth environment, not just accept what we have and continue to abuse it. The human family has enormous resources—wealth, wisdom, scientific understanding, and the capability through public and private channels to create a healthy earth environment. The trick, of course, is to use the resources of both governmental agencies and private industry in a constructive way to change the current pattern of self-serving behavior and exploitation.

It has been encouraging to see several world leaders of government agencies and private enterprise meeting together to address the threats to the total earth environment, not just one small segment. There is growing acceptance of the reality that this is a global issue, one that must be addressed collaboratively, not exclusively in one domain or locale. The goal is to create an *earth* community, not just a European or North American region with ecological integrity.

We ask, of course, what is meant by the goal of creating an earth environment with "ecological integrity"? Implied in this statement is that all of life on earth is valued and is sustained by the resources of the earth. Therefore, our practices of utilizing the resources of the earth to sustain and improve life must be done in a way that preserves them, not just for a brief period, but also well into the future for coming generations. We must learn how to change patterns and practices in which the earth is exploited by self-serving ends, those with power and wealth, and even national governments. We engage in this process in a way that honors the value of all of life and finds ways to sustain the resources that both conserve and preserve life. Our use of the earth's resources must have integrity while sustaining and improving life well into the future. And it is not just human life that needs to be sustained in a positive way, but we need a clear recognition that all of life is interrelated and has value. *Our policies and practices must be in harmony with* (have integrity with) *our deep belief in the inherent value of life.*

Our immediate challenges and tasks in the fulfillment of this objective include the following:[5]

1. overconsumption, in situations where the uses of resources outpace the sustainable capacity of the ecosystem;

2. overpopulation, where there are too many people for the planet to sustain and too many people in certain regions where it has already reached the crisis point;

---

5. https://en.wikipedia.org/wiki/list-of-global-issues. I have modestly altered the lists to provide clarity. I do acknowledge there is some repetition, but it is a risk taken in an effort to explain more clearly.

Compassionate Spirituality

3. biodiversity loss, threatening the balance and sustainability of a region;
4. deforestation, threatening the habitats and climates in certain regions;
5. desertification, again threatening the habitats of large populations and the loss of the food resources to sustain them;
6. global warming and climate change as a summary of what we are facing;
7. habitat destruction, underlined with deforestation and desertification;
8. Holocene extinction (the collapse of the present epoch), ignoring the current situation and creating new and threatening situations;
9. pollution: waste and waste disposal, water pollution;
10. resource depletion at all levels;
11. urban sprawl, creating poverty and unsafe conditions.

These challenges, related to creating and sustaining an earth environment with ecological integrity, suggest the third major goal of the United Nations. It is "to create a global culture of social and economic justice." The problems we face as an earth community are interwoven, and our failure to understand and solve these problems impacts the governmental and financial stability of many countries of the world. This instability underlines the need to create a global culture of social and economic justice. The following challenges underline the urgency of this third goal:

1. lack of food security, especially for developing countries, but also to some extent it exists in developed countries;
2. lack of inclusive growth of resources benefiting all people, again not just for the "haves" but also and especially for those who have limited education and less access to the food and housing;
3. future of work and the risks of unemployment in settings where there is a specialized and complex economic context, one very difficult to navigate;
4. climate change that makes life very difficult to sustain, especially for the poor in certain regions of the world;
5. the possibility of a global financial crisis (one was present in 2007–2008) that impacts the poor and even those without accumulated wealth;
6. the future of information technology that does not benefit all people as it becomes increasingly more complex, and the presence and use of the Internet as our "industrial revolution";

7. lack of gender and racial equality as countries struggle to deal with the range of challenging conditions;
8. global trade and investment and regulatory frameworks that may not ensure justice for all;
9. long-term investment policies and strategy that do not benefit all people;
10. future healthcare that may not be available to all people.

Again, we need to emphasize that governmental agencies, private wealth, and corporate businesses must join forces to create legal pathways and accessible programs to enable all citizens to have access to the earth's resources. As I write, in that the earth has sufficient resources to serve the people of the world, the motivation of those with abundant wealth must be changed to focus on the welfare of all people, not just the protection of their way of life. This shift should not necessarily be termed as *socialism* or *communism*, language often used by those who oppose the goal and suggests distortions of what is meant by the goal. It is true that there is a profound need for government involvement, but no suggestion of the particular form of government that can achieve these goals. In short, it must be a compassionate response that will improve the welfare of all people and provide a safe environment for all. A more equitable distribution of wealth and live-sustaining resources will make a safer and better world for all. Further, government structures must find avenues of efficient distribution of resources to ensure the welfare of the people whom they serve. A more equitable distribution system is a constant challenge, often filled with poor planning and political controversy, but the creation of a global culture of social and economic justice is not just a nice dream of caring do-gooders. Rather, it is a global goal that is a necessity for a sustainable earth community. All will suffer and are suffering without it.

A fourth goal of the United Nations *Earth Charter* follows from the third; it is the creation of a global context of democracy, nonviolence, and peace. This goal follows directly from the third goal, the creation of a global culture of social and economic justice. Even a brief reading of history will tell us that where there is no opportunity for people to participate in shaping one's governmental policies and practices and no chance to shape one's own future, there will be resistance to those in power, and actions taken in this resistance often lead to violence. It is a democratic form of government in which there is the involvement of people in shaping their future (the vote) that will ensure social and economic justice. The presence of social and economic justice will reduce if not eliminate violence and lead to peace. Those favoring an autocracy where there are limited opportunities to shape one's future often argue that they (those in power) know better how to manage the challenges of a stable government and a thriving country. Often hidden behind this argument is the quest for power and the opportunity to gain wealth. Putin may be one the wealthiest people in the world, yet there is poverty and unrest in Russia. Admittedly, the Chinese do have complex challenges in governance given the size of their population, yet one sees some of the same challenges being managed in the nearby huge nation of India, which values a democratic form of government. Governing large countries is very difficult!

Recent developments in the United States, while incredibly hard to unpack and understand, do suggest the larger truth that peace is dependent on social and economic justice, globally of course, but also nationally and regionally. Democratic forms of government committed to finding nonviolent means to achieve their goals result in peaceful states. New Zealand may be one of the best examples of this historical reality, although it does have a smaller population, yet still manages to maintain its democratic practices with a minority and indigenous population. One example of the wisdom of their form of government is the way they led the world in the management of the COVID-19, having the lowest percentage of those who became ill from the global pandemic.

I do wish that the United States had done as well in the early stages of the pandemic, but in time the US did achieve many of its goals in preventing the spread of the disease, and did so in what might be characterized in the broadest sense as a method that was democratic in design and implementation. It did not respond as well in the early stages, in part because of the accumulation of power in the office of the president and his refusal or inability to manage such a complex problem. Toward the end of the Trump presidency and still present in right-wing politics, there is the assumption that democracy doesn't work; and even the word *compassion* has become a dangerous word for those who are committed to right-wing extremism.

Heather Cox Richardson, a noted history scholar and writer, using the wording of one hundred scholars, directly warns that "our entire democracy is at risk."[6] She demonstrates the ways that new election laws in Republican-led states passed with the justification that they will make elections safer, threaten the democratic principles upon which our government

---

6. Richardson, *Letters from an American*, June 1, 2021. She is often a much-needed "voice crying in the wilderness."

was founded. She goes on to maintain that if we permit the breakdown of our democracy by making it more difficult to vote, it will be very difficult to reverse the damage. Implied in her argument is that voting should not be dependent on the restrictive policies of the party that controls the state government, but the state should use the same method for all citizens, regardless of party affiliation. In the *United* States, all votes should be cast and counted equally in all of the states. Since her thoughtful article, we have observed that strange and chaotic way that right-wing extremists in Arizona have attempted to audit and change the way that the election for the president of the United States takes place. The beliefs and claims of those calling for yet another audit seem unfounded and extreme.[7]

What has happened in the United States, and continues to happen as I write,[8] is also occurring in other countries with autocratic governments.[9] The United Nations charter's goal that we must seek the creation of a global context of democracy, nonviolence, and peace is as important now if not more important as in 2000.

One might ask why there is a concern about the advocacy of a global context for democratic governments that engage in creating a context that is nonviolent and peaceful, as well as the commitment to the other three goals in the United Nations *Earth Charter*. The clear and straightforward answer is that these goals are a way of insuring the well-being of human life and the future of all life on earth. They express transcendent values that are universal in history. They are the best way forward regardless of whether they are the product of evolutionary development, the unfolding of history, or built into reality by a divine hand. They are an expression of compassionate and inclusive ways of governance without reference to a personal God, although a religious person might say that these values represent the deep religious belief in a Divine One who calls upon the human family to seek the welfare of all of life and the well-being of Mother Earth. We turn now to an exploration of the range of contemporary options of finding a way into the future, perhaps traces of Transcendence that suggest and affirm these values and point to a more universal frame of reference.

---

7. Or off the wall.
8. July 2021.
9. Turkey is but one example.

9

Contemporary Options and Finding a Pathway

WISE CHOICES

I HAVE TRIED TO lay a foundation for making good decisions about selecting a spiritual pathway and finding wise ways of moving forward on the basis of what we consider to be traces of transcendence and even glimpses of Transcendence. What we hope is that these traces and glimpses point us to an accurate picture of reality and provide foundations for possible spiritual pathways that are credible, healthy, and life-giving. As we seek to find such a spiritual pathway, we hope there will be reliable glimpses of Ultimate Reality, often grasped and experienced in a faith relationship. Finding and connecting with Transcendence is the heart of the spiritual quest. So we have used the term *transcendence*, where in lowercase it refers to the reality that we encounter as we undertake the tasks of our daily responsibilities and as we manage a given day (transcendence). We also use the term with a capital T to suggest that there are traces and glimpses that point to the source and ground of all reality (Transcendence), and it is from this Source and Presence that we find guidance for our deepest values, for life's direction and purpose, and for eternal rest.

Section Three: The Current Practices of Spirituality

By these terms *transcendence* and *Transcendence* we have maintained that our lives are shaped and guided sometimes by conscious awareness and sometimes by unconscious assumptions, forces, principles, and undergirding realities, which form the context in which we live. They are the foundation upon which "we live, move, and have our being."[1] We discern traces of these transcendent realities and we make the assumption that these traces and glimpses are a solid foundation for our beliefs, decisions, and actions. As we understand them more fully, they guide us in life, and therefore we hope that we are able to discern them clearly and become aware of their influence. To move toward and experience the good and healthy life, we must continually live in tune with those *traces* of ultimate reality that intersect with our lives.

It is wise to be self-aware and even self-critical about our assumptions and prior understanding, because we know how easy it is to misread the signals of transcendent realities. We want and need to be congruent people with integrity, living in harmony with reality. And we know that when we do not have a clear view of reality, our decisions can lead us astray and be quite harmful. We want to go forward in life on the basis of having an increasingly accurate understanding of the reality that surrounds us. We want to base our decisions about our personal lives, the way we undertake our daily tasks, and the way we organize our social and governmental systems on what we hope are an accurate understanding about the foundations of the path we walk, the decisions we make, and the dreams we have about our future. We launch out to construct our patterns of life, as we might construct a home or a bridge, on the basis of what we consider to be safe and solid foundations. Both transcendence and Transcendence come into play.

I thought it might be wise to illustrate these foundational principles in my life, as a way of grasping them more personally. As the chapter unfolds, I will begin to give illustrations of how I have walked this spiritual path, and I hope these personal illustrations will bring these concerns closer to our center, our spiritual home.

We have tried to describe how, across time and in a religious context, humans have built their homes and bridges, and their personal, social, spiritual, and corporate lives, on what they believe they can trust as truthful and reliable foundations. They want an accurate understanding of transcendental realities, those with a small t and those with a capital T. We say, for example, "I believe in a personal God" (Transcendent Presence or

---

1. Acts 17:28.

Source) and hope it is well-placed trust in an accurate reading of traces of Transcendence. Perhaps with a slightly different kind of trust and confidence, we learn from transcendence; it is our reading of our environment, and we find guidance by careful testing, study, and reflection.

THE PRESENCE OF CONFLICT

On occasion, these two ways of understanding reality, transcendence and Transcendence, cause some internal conflicts and disagreements with others. These conflicts can be harmful, create personal discomfort, and separate us from others. Fortunately, many of us have found good ways of dealing with these conflicting views of reality within our own lives and with others. It can be especially difficult with others because all too often the first impulse is to oppose the views of the other person or group, and as we do we may inadvertently create conflict that deepens the separation rather than heals it. It can cause deep frustration and nearly stop us from moving forward in life. Internal conflicts are not easy to resolve either, and we often live with two voices or more within us. As one who has served as a chaplain and pastor, I have counseled many people who are distressed by the deep conflict within. But with a good measure of self-acceptance, and then kindness, patience, empathy, we can begin to overcome distressful conflicts. With an insightful self-understanding, an appreciation of the complexity of conflict in others, and the passing of time, the threat is reduced and we find acceptable ways to resolve both internal and external conflicts. Gradually we move toward just accepting that there will be differences of understanding and recognizing that having different views is acceptable and often makes for a more creative environment. And, better yet, we find ways to integrate these conflicting perspectives by adjusting our views to a more accurate and deeper reading of reality, one that brings inner peace and joyful relationship with others.

In the spiritual realm, the Christian faith (the expression of religion I know best) provides us with an endless number of cases of the adjustment of views and their integration as a means of managing conflict.[2] For example, there is the well-known modification of beliefs to accommodate to the new

---

2. See the masterful and comprehensive study of Christian belief and practice, Jaroslav Pelican's five- volume work *The Christian Tradition: A History of the Development of Doctrine*. A major part of the story is the quest to resolved differences of belief and practice.

scientific evidence of the sun-centered universe rather than an earth-centered universe, although it took a long time for the church to adjust. Careful study and scientific understanding have forced the church to be open to new understandings of reality and incorporate better ways of understanding human consciousness, the world around us, and guiding universal values. And the Christian church, although not without stress, has become a much better institution as it has adjusted its views to scientific and postmodern understanding when dealing with a range of issues. New and more accurate ways of reading reality are not really the enemy, but our friends.

It is often the case, as it has been with the church, that we are unaware of what we are assuming because it has become the norm in our immediate setting and our culture. Without self-reflection, we just accept the way those in our segment of the world understand reality and follow common patterns of thought and action. It is assumed that the undergirding principles shared by the majority of those in our culture are the basis of what is true and show us the way to making wise decisions. Unfortunately, our outlook is not always an accurate perception of reality, and, hopefully, with a good measure of self-reflection, we move forward in good faith and modify our views and prior understanding, knowing that new information and perspectives will provide us with a more credible foundation. Yet many of our questions, debates, and conflicts continue and often revolve around our assumed outlooks, that what we see and affirm are accurate perceptions. Then, as there is conflict, we continually say that what others who disagree with us see and believe is not the case or at least not totally accurate. Some disagreement may be healthy and serve us well by providing the motivation to carefully study the cause of the conflict and help us find positive ways of resolving conflict. All too frequently, however, fear and threat enter in, and we are unable to see clearly the truth that may be in an opposing view. When this happens, we end up without the resolution of differences.

As one who has spent some time in university settings, a culture of questions and debate, I have grown increasingly humble about my abilities to always know the truth and how easily I assume because of my mindset that I have the truth. I then tend to impose it on that which I am trying to understand. I have also learned to respect and honor those who know more than I do about a given subject. I have learned to listen carefully and struggle to understand and modify my views. In addition, I have learned ways to have a constructive debate and know that deepening my knowledge is more important than winning an argument. I have gained some

Contemporary Options and Finding a Pathway

patience and am slower to judge what others believe and say, knowing that assumptions about Transcendence and transcendence are often hidden in the discussion.[3]

As I have continued to search for truthful ways to describe certain subjects (realities), I have developed some principles that guide what I say, write, and how I make decisions. I learn from Einstein that "the more I know, the more I know I don't know." For example:

1. I begin with a measure of humility about my grasp of the issue or concern. Therefore, before I make the decision or undertake the task, I reflect on the reality that I may not have sufficient information; I pause so that my decision will not be exclusively based on my presuppositions and assumptions. Having learned the hard way many times, I am now more apt to do careful study of the subject about which I speak or write and about those moments in which I have to make a hard decision. I pause to learn more in order to engage constructively in making a difficult decision or undertaking a complex task.

2. I often set a more limited goal of what I want to accomplish as I make a case for my point of view or describe the basis of the action I am about to take. Generally, I take some little steps forward, try to gain more knowledge and an informed outlook, knowing that major life decisions or descriptions of big-picture subjects are hard to grasp fully and to prove because of their complexity; they are often, unfortunately, described and defended by hidden presuppositions that are assumed and have not been examined.

3. I try to be self-conscious about the assumptions in my outlook and how I view reality. I know that I move forward with the understanding of transcendence of my time and place in history, the cultural norms that surround me, and the flow of my life and personal beliefs. I am who I am and feel good about it, but I know that I cannot always generalize about difficult subjects and issues from my experience and outlook. It is hard to describe an elephant, the blind man learned, by just touching its tail or one part of the giant creature such as the tip of the trunk. It might be a mouse.

3. My dissertation and first book (*Biblical Hermeneutics*) was based on "preunderstanding" in biblical interpretation, a very lively context for claiming truth without awareness of hidden assumptions. German New Testament scholar Rudolf Bultmann maintained the prior understanding shapes our reading of the Bible and our understanding of Jesus. I argued with him in my dissertation, but I think he may have won.

Section Three: The Current Practices of Spirituality

4. I try to be especially aware of what assumptions about transcendence or Transcendence are operative in my thinking, my speaking, in my writing, and my daily walk, knowing that I will be influenced by their presence. For the most part, I try to honor what I consider to be important foundations and affirmations, especially in the areas of religious belief and guiding values. So, I'll not give up on the priority of loving others, but tend rethink and change the ways of doing it. To humbly acknowledge this reality gives me a measure of humility and honesty, both necessary as we seek to understand and act wisely and well.

5. Religious beliefs are especially challenging in this regard. They are quite complex, and often assumed to be true on faith rather than based on reason and critical study, which they can only partially be. And they profoundly shape our way of life, and of course our relationships. But a good measure of humility here is in order as well; it is our faith that moves us toward having at least a partial understanding of universal truth, but it will be approximate.

6. I look for what may be classified as truthful foundational assumptions, such as well-reasoned and logical arguments and what thoughtful and well-educated people say about a particular subject. I look for accurate descriptions based on careful observation and study, pay attention to my own personal integrity as far possible, and avoid resting my view on my own insecurities, needs, and self-serving attitudes and statements. I then examine with care the ground or basis of my beliefs. I do acknowledge the sense of immediate intimacy and knowing, as in the case of a mystical experience of the Divine, yet I remain cautious when people describe these experiences. They may be talking about their parent rather than their divine Parent.

So I plunge into life, trying as far as possible, with my relatively good education and a developing pattern of maintaining an open mind, to avoid hidden prejudice and ignorance. I hope that if it is present, it might be discovered early on and discarded. I seek to be wise in discerning how what I say and do might be heard or interpreted, and as far possible, making sure that what I say and do will serve the common good. These principles and other factors such as the unique nature of the subject guide me in the exploration of traces of transcendence and the actions I take because of them. On the basis of these principles, I suggest the following pattern as we seek to find a way to move forward in our daily lives and in our spiritual pathway:

Contemporary Options and Finding a Pathway

1. Act with as *full an understanding* as possible of the traces of transcendence and the glimpses of Transcendence in the concern, the issue, or course of action. Ask what is being suggested by prior assumptions and assumed in our statements about reality, the decisions we make, and the actions we take. On what foundation do we plan to move forward? How can we build a safe bridge? Or a credible faith?

2. Be sure to *carefully select* and be clear about what type of transcendence is foundational for the subject I want to describe, the decision I need to make, or the course of action I plan to take. I do start with assumptions, and I can make choices about principles and priorities that guide me. As I speak, for example, am I seeking attention and affirmation or am I trying to share information that will be helpful in managing the tasks ahead? I ask, what is the motivation behind what I am saying or doing? Have I assumed too much or chosen the wrong direction and missed or only partially understood the nature of the foundations of what I am thinking and saying?

3. Be as thoughtful and as informed as possible in *integrating, linking,* and *relating* your understanding of transcendence, and especially in reference to Transcendence, with the best expressions of a contemporary knowledge. Not that your beliefs can't challenge the predominant worldview of our time; it may and usually does need challenge and redirection. You may challenge a contemporary view, and great minds and saintly hearts have done so, but do it for the right reasons, not just to further your own self-serving ends. Be sure you understand as well as Copernicus or Darwin and care as much as Gandhi or Mother Teresa. For example, what might the relationship be between Augustine's view or original sin and contemporary views of human evolution? Should we rest exclusively on ancient Greek metaphysics that assume all things have a unique *substance* in our quest to understand the human and the divine in Jesus, or should w find more contemporary ways of understanding this remarkable human being?

I want to expand on these three suggested patterns as we move forward toward a better understanding of the traces of transcendence and Transcendence and their place in our lives. I will continue to be somewhat autobiographical and personal in my description of how I have attempted to follow these three patterns of behavior. Perhaps my experience, as flawed as it has been, will still cross over to the experience of readers and be helpful in the quest to live an informed, healthy, and responsible life.

GAINING A FULL UNDERSTANDING

I begin by pointing to the ways I have attempted to gain as much understanding as possible about finding my way of reading the traces of transcendence, and in my case, the glimpses of Transcendence. On what prior understanding and foundational principles have I attempted to gain a better understanding of how to live in an authentic and congruent way with reality? And what steps have I taken to understand and connect with the Source and Presence if my quest is to find a spiritual path? Over the years of daily responsibility and decision-making, I do believe I have made some progress in gaining an informed and critical understanding of the world around me, and I have recognized the place of transcendence as very important in this endeavor. I have gained some skills and a measure of wisdom, have become more self-aware, and have learned about the culture and context in which I live. Reading widely has been a great help. I have carefully reviewed the ways that my family life and broader experience of my early years have shaped the person I have become. I have reflected on the context of my early life, the family I inherited, the culture in which I grew up, the country in which I lived, and the education I received. I have tried to get in touch with how my life took shape, understand the values and goals I inherited and refined, and why I am now the adult that I am. As I have understood more, I have begun to accept that I am all right, but hardly perfect and have a few more miles to go before I sleep.

While I did not grow up in a religiously oriented home, I did find a way into a religious outlook and pattern of life. I initially accepted its presence in somewhat uncritical ways in high school, yet took it seriously, and in time it became a more informed and it nudged me toward a more mature outlook and way of life. Because of these early exposures and commitments, I choose to focus my education in the field of religious studies, initially to prepare myself for a career in ministry, and in time a career in higher education with the field of religious studies as my base. Those of us who are scholars in the field of religious studies know that religion may be studied in critical and historical ways, and my education in the field helped me to set aside some idiosyncratic and even exclusive, cultic, and tribal beliefs and practices. I was invited into a religious outlook that was based

Contemporary Options and Finding a Pathway

more on truth-seeking, inclusive and compassionate behavior, and a social conscience that motivated me to lend a hand in creating a more just and peaceful world.

I also became aware that when I begin to describe a belief in Transcendence, I moved into slightly different intellectual territory. Knowledge about religion and its place in the world were extremely helpful in shaping my outlook, but it didn't take me to the point of personal connection and commitment. Learning about what people taught *about* God was important, but it didn't connect me with God. Part of what I learned about the term *God* was that any God worthy of commitment and worship, if understood in a profound way, is not a thing or another floating object in space, but is beyond our capacity to fully explain and classify. Our language and thought are not sufficiently adequate to describe God, but they do point us in a direction and teach us that our God is too small if we think we can tame God with our limited knowledge and patterns of thought. What we mean by *God* does not fit into the easy categories of cause and effect and careful description or into our limited views early in faith journey. We can describe the nature of belief, the views that have been held, and the different ways God has been understood, but it is generally thought that to describe God as one more object in the world of objects is not to describe God at all, although various beliefs in God can be studied in this way. But we mean something different when we speak of God as eternal, omnipresent, and omnipotent—not our categories as we first begin on a spiritual path. We need to learn how to speak of the Transcendence that stands behind it all and only gives us glimpses and traces, some of which we hope are a true revelation.

So, for us to gain a full understanding the role of Transcendence, we must openly acknowledge that our belief in God will have to move us into a different realm of understanding. We move into the realm of faith and begin the task of saying yes or no on the basis of the traces and glimpses because we can't fully arrive there with limited understanding or with well-reasoned arguments and scientific inquiry. In my case, I was introduced concurrently both to traces of transcendence and to glimpses of Transcendence. I valued the small t, learning about the underlying scientific explanations of the formation and functioning of the cosmos, and how my relatively small world worked. I liked understanding myself better and understanding the world in which I lived. I had a good measure of curiosity. Yet I also had some needs; that is, I wasn't totally secure and self-contained and needed to understand how I came to be, and what the causes were for my levels of both security and insecurity, of inner peace and anxiety, and levels of confidence or lack of it in my relationships, roles in life, and my sense of selfhood. I wanted and needed to understand, and the study of small-t transcendence was a great gift. But these needs invited me to be open to the capital T, finding a satisfying and an enlightened understanding and commitment to follow the will and way of God. I sensed a need for a ray of light, a pattern of life to follow that gave guidance to my values and empowered me to engage in a way of life based on love, compassion, justice, and peace. The capital-T Transcendence became a personal connection, a sense of not only being loved but also being guided to a life of meaning and service.

Fortunately, I was able to secure a good education, found wonderful ways to explain the roller coaster of feelings and thoughts, and was usually accepted by others. I found a fairly good place in my somewhat dysfunctional family, my associations, and the world around me. I went through the several stages of human development and faith development, although not easily, which turned out to be a kind of plus in that it motivated the quest for self-understanding and big-picture understanding. As time went along, I realized that my understanding was rooted in my family life, my culture in middle-class America, and my time in history, from World War II to postmodernism with all of its strange twists and turns.

I found a base in Christianity and a model in the life and teachings of Jesus. At first, it was a fairly innocent sense of Transcendence and acceptance of what I was taught. Through graduate studies in religion, my base barely survived, yet it did and became much more nuanced and complex, and I found a good measure of freedom to roam around in the world of theology and religious studies. And, with much more critical reflection, I hung on to the teaching that God was love and light (truth) and that Jesus epitomized love and light; he was "full of grace and truth" (John 1:14). I innocently affirmed this belief in high school and affirm it now at the tail of end of life; that God is both *present* and *beyond*, and I rest in this sense of Transcendence.

CAREFULLY SELECTING

I gained as full an understanding as possible of this place that gave me peace, grateful that my life, education, and experiences made it possible. The more I know about the ways Transcendence has been understood, the less sure I am that I can describe it in a clear and simple way, but it continues

Contemporary Options and Finding a Pathway

be the center from which most other aspects of my life flow. I meet many others who have different patterns of affirming or denying Transcendence, and I honor them and often learn from them. As I go through the process of assessing the place where my parachute has landed, I look at the spot with great care and then observe where others in the human family have also landed. Let me summarize what I feel and notice as vitally important as I now fold my parachute. I see many broad concerns that we should be sensitive to as we fold our parachutes and move forward. I want to stress four deep concerns, in part because they have been troubling for me, although there are many others that could be mentioned. I sense that we need to factor in these concerns as we develop and affirm a belief in Transcendence if it is to be credible and a trustworthy foundation, more than just a superstitious and popular cultural norm.

1. I both feel and see an enormous amount of *suffering* around me, and that any selection of a foundation on which to build my life should be conscious of this reality and deal with it wisely as one shapes foundational religious beliefs. There are several reasons I urge this awareness, two of which I want to underline. The first is that any understanding of the Divine or God needs to ask why, if God is all loving and all-powerful, God does not remove evil and suffering from the world. This concern remains the greatest roadblock to a belief in a loving God. The second is that if one just accepts not having a final answer to the first question, which I do, does one's faith in God or Transcendence carry with it the ethical mandate to care for those who suffer in all of its many diabolical forms. There are many who have jumped and landed and can't fold their parachutes. They have landed, some in healthy settings, but many in terrible settings. This picture underlines for me the reality of human suffering and that all suffering must be understood, dealt with, and factored into my understanding of why I jumped, where I landed, what I believe, and what I need to and should do.

2. The second concern has to do with the many different kinds of people who are present as I land. There is great *diversity*. They have a great many beliefs and have a broad range of experience. Many are thoughtful and enlightened, yet have quite different views than I have. Some believe in a form of Transcendence, while many others don't. Those with a belief in Transcendence may have a view quite different from mine, and yet it gives them an understanding of their identity and

values, what to believe, and what to do next. Others, unsure about Transcendence, share the same transcendence and have all kinds of explanations of the world, where they came from, and how they should live their lives. I need to ask whether their beliefs and ethical practices are just as valid as mine. Do I dare say that my beliefs are correct and their beliefs are wrong? What gives me the right to be exclusive, especially if I exclude others with different beliefs and practices? Have my religious beliefs and practices become sectarian, cultic, and tribal?

3. As I look around, I see that there is great diversity of beliefs, but also of practice. Without exception, our *practices*, as well founded and compassionate as they may be, *are still identified and formed out of our culture and time in place in history.* Those from different cultures were given different instructions and guidance about what to do in life and what resources one needs to find one's way. Their parachutes were folded in a different way. The airplanes were different sizes, came from different countries, had different destinations, and gave a variety of instructions on how to live when you land. India Airlines informed their parachutists with different assumptions and directions than Pakistan Airlines. American Airlines informed their jumpers with different reason for the flight and its mission than Kenya Airlines. Those who landed from different airlines still believe firmly in what they were taught and tend to see the world and their lives from this perspective. Is their outlook, different from mine, then faulty?

4. Another concern about making universal claims about my understanding of Transcendence that we must face is the reality that *many belief systems are fading away.* There is a huge group of people who do not see much evidence for or guidance from a transcendent other, but have learned about and *accepted the reality of what is happening around them and view the world through the lens of scientific rationalism.* These people have found ways to fold their parachutes with little external guidance. They learned about the country and the plane, found ways to live in a constructive manner, carefully observed how to live in the setting and good ways of living together, and were able to cope and relieve the suffering of others. It is enough to understand what happened, where they were, and what to do. There are guiding principles of living together in wise ways, providing care for those who suffer, and creating the best possible way of life. They see no evidence

or reason to suggest there is a transcendent other that stands behind it all, provides purpose and meaning, and teaches about the good and ethical life. It is all there in front of them and can be understood with a quality education, respect for others, getting together, and implementing patterns of living together based on the principles of justice and peace. It is possible to learn the best ways of life from past experience in the airplane, the realities of parachuting, and what is present in the place where we landed. Then simply say, "Let's get organized and put it together." Do we really need a deep belief in Transcendence now that we understand all that exists in a scientific, evolutionary, and developmental frame of reference?

THE PROCESS OF INTEGRATION

I'll not try to provide a Transcendent outlook that deals directly with these four concerns, but they will be in the background as we attempt to make our belief system credible and acceptable in contemporary life. The way to undertake this task is to integrate it into the way the world is now understood, which is a bit hard to summarize with a label, but we might say that it is secular, based on historical, rational, and scientific understanding. It is also true that there is great variety and much that is based on positive religious outlooks, but also a great deal of ignorance, superstition, and unhealthy prejudice. Yet I would suggest that it would be accurate to say that the contemporary worldview is essentially based on a secular understanding of reality. There are great risks in ignoring and rejecting a rational and scientific understanding of reality. If we don't take it into account, our views will not be germane in the world we inhabit, although a critical perspective on the contemporary worldview still has its place. But if we just reject it, we will become historical castoffs.

As we move to modify and update our understanding of Transcendence, we discover the need to integrate it into what science and reason tell us. It brings great value to our understanding of Transcendence if we are able to integrate it with a contemporary view of reality. Of course, not all contemporary people will need to explain their chosen way of life; it is enough to live each day with some enjoyment and pleasant circumstances. But some of us, if our views guide others, contend that it is important to be intentional about life, to be sure that what guides us about the deeper dimensions of life is based on our best understanding of reality and upon as much of the truth that we can discern. We feel called to find deeper purpose and meaning in life in reference to that truth, especially as we guide others who assume than just having enough food, sleep, and friends for day-to-day living is enough. We protect against the suffering that occurs when life does not have an authentic foundation. Hitler did not have an accurate view of reality, and his false consciousness caused suffering beyond description. Some current views have a trace of Hitler's movement in Germany in the 1930s and 1940s.

So, with diligence and integrity, we need to ask how it is possible to live in harmony with what we know is an accurate understanding of reality, and we should be ready to help those who ask with well-founded and persuasive answers. It is my view that we should never live with a false consciousness, elevating that which is untrue to place of universal value. It is a pervasive practice in our time, and I have become disillusioned by its presence. For example, many of our government leaders have accepted what has been called *the big lie* about the results of the 2020 presidential election. This cynical quest for power shifts our form of governance from one based on truth to one based on falsehood. It is but one way that we are beginning to lean as a culture toward using falsehood in the quest for power and control. In my judgment, it is an enormous threat to our way of life.

Rather, we should build the foundations of our government on truth, and then seek to live intelligently, ethically, and in accord with the values of goodness, truth, and beauty. At this point in our history, we need to sense that deep inside ourselves that the unexamined life is not worth living and even dangerous. It is the examined life that will guide us to live authentically and with integrity. We need to ask whether there are universal principles that guide one to a good life, ones based on truth and filled with the purpose of making life better, not only for us but also for those in our circle of nearness. We need to study and carefully reflect about transcendence and Transcendence and make wise and truthful choices about what to believe and how to live.

One possible way to speak about finding a good way to live with integrity that has wide appeal is the one suggested by Plato: that our lives should be filled with goodness, truth, and beauty, understood as transcendent values based on universal truth that has the capacity to cross historical eras and different cultures. Others, such as Buddha, Moses, Jesus, and Mohammad, place more emphasis on Transcendence, although Buddha's sense of

Contemporary Options and Finding a Pathway

Transcendence was not tied to a personal God. I want to draw a possible picture of the good life, learning from the great teachers of spiritual wisdom, using the categories that have been suggested, but expanding on them and suggesting ways to integrate our beliefs, often rooted in history, with a more contemporary worldview. The goal is to find values and patterns of life that are congruent with our understanding of reality and our identity, which point us in the direction of improving the condition of all those who continue to jump out of airplanes and land in conditions that are not always comfortable and supportive.

FOUNDATIONS: TRUTH, LOVE, JUSTICE, AND PEACE

Again, being somewhat personal, I want to suggest as a short summary that our lives should be based on the foundational values of truth, love, justice, and peace. I begin with truth, wanting once again to underline its importance and to affirm that an essential part of our hope is the belief that the good life is based on living truthfully. Once again, we approach transcendence and Transcendence. We speak about being an honest person who tells the truth and lives an authentic life, a life with integrity. In addition, as we approach this issue of truth, we also approach the issue of Transcendence and ask whether it makes sense in our day and age to say that is possible to understand and encounter the very foundation of truth, and have a credible belief in the Divine, what we understand to be a personal God. It may not be necessary to root our understanding of truth in Transcendence, and I do pay attention to this point of view. Yet I find comfort in believing that God is light and truth.

There has been and continues to be a debate about the existence of God, and it is a question that will likely continue to be with us.[4] It is not easy to continue to be a believer in that much of contemporary knowledge and understanding do point us in other directions. While there are many—and I am one of them—who find it difficult to believe in God, especially as God has been perceived in simplistic ways, there are many thoughtful people who still firmly believe in a personal Transcendence on which to base their values, and this belief has been affirmed with many contemporary arguments for the existence of God.

---

4. For example, there were several books in the last few decades that took aim at religious belief in the existence of God. Among them were Hitchens, *god Is Not Great*; Harris, *End of Faith*; Bloom, *God Problem*; and Dawkins, *God Delusion*.

Section Three: The Current Practices of Spirituality

Among them is the thoughtful and persuasive book by David Bentley Hart, *The Experience of God: Being, Consciousness, Bliss*.[5] His point of view has a contemporary ring and points us in the direction of integration with a more contemporary outlook without the rejection of a belief in God. He urges the reader to move in a direction of credible belief rather than in a defensive and fear-based rejection of a secular, rational, scientific outlook.[6]

In part because of my university teaching and pastoral responsibilities, I have found time to read most of these more positive attempts at the integration of transcendence and Transcendence with some care. It is not altogether easy to summarize the arguments, but a brief summary might provide at least a place to start public discussion and private reflection. The arguments for the existence God as a foundation for universal values have generally take three directions, and these are present in both the historical arguments and the contemporary arguments.[7]

The first direction, taken by such fine scholars as Hans Küng and Richard Swinburne, is that a careful statement of belief in God matches with one of the main requirements of a truth statement: that it must be logical and coherent, offering a comprehensive argument that makes sense and carefully refutes the claim that belief in God is illogical and does not measure up to the requirements of the current tests for truth. These authors and several others have carefully stated the basis for belief in God in a way that fulfills the requirement that any statement of truth must be logical and coherent. People such as Richard Dawkins and Sam Harris say that this positive point of view does not prove that there is a God, only that a coherent case can be made for belief in God, and that a case could also be made about most anything, even the existence of fairies. Yet to make arguments for the existence of God in reasonable, logical, and coherent ways gets the subject into the discussion. An intelligent case for belief in God can be made.

Those making the case for belief in God do acknowledge that logical coherence is but one foundational point, and then add another vital part of the argument: that a thoughtful belief in God does have the capacity to help

---

5. Others included Allen, *Traces of God*; McIntosh, *Presence of the Infinite*; Swinburne, *Coherence of Theism*; and Küng, *Does God Exist*.

6. The work of Ken Wilbur is far more extensive, more inclusive, and less traditional than Hart's, and perhaps the most persuasive view in the defense of a spiritual outlook, although not a defense of Christian or traditional monotheism.

7. Any summary will inevitably oversimplify and miss part of the arguments, but getting the tone and spirit of the arguments might lend a helpful perspective.

us understand and explain the cause and character of so much that exists. Belief in God makes sense in a metaphysical way in that it demonstrates the reason why and suggests the how about the entire scope of the universe and all of reality.[8] Again, those opposed to belief say that this argument doesn't point to a personal God, but only an observation that the reality we know has a discernable order and rhythm. People such as Einstein pondered this question. The response, of course, is that to use the belief in God to answer why there is order and rhythm in the universe is not proof of the existence of God, or more directly, does not prove that there is a personal and loving God. Yet the proposition that such a God stands behind it all does offer one defensible point of view.

A third dimension of the argument for the existence of God has to do with human experience. A relatively recent illustration of this argument is contained in the book already mentioned, David Bentley Hart's *The Experience of God*.[9] Hart's argument is logical and coherent, yes, but almost more to the point is his affirmation that the very fact of being itself, human consciousness, and the ultimately gratifying experience of bliss are persuasive arguments for the existence of a personal God. It is able to demonstrate more than just the obvious point that there had to be a first push made by a divine being to explain how it all started. There are clear pointers to a God of love, purpose, and beauty.[10] Where else might these experiences have originated? I am a natural doubter, but Hart's arguments enable me to lean toward believing, and when I arrive, I generally find that my expectations are met. I find deep fulfillment in the way I have folded my parachute, although continue to wonder and grow in the process.

A second part of the way I have tried to fold my parachute is to make love and its cousin, compassion, central to what I believe and the way I live my life. The initial component of the test for truth, that a statement must be logical and coherent, is important, but a second test is equally important: that what we claim to believe must ring true in the most mature expressions of human experience. This test isn't always germane in a truth test, and some statements of truth have no emotional content. But a belief in

---

8. Küng's arguments are very thorough and persuasive in *Does God Exist*, 552–83.

9. David Christopher, in his book *The Holy Universe: A New Story of Creation for the Heart, Soul, and Spirit*, argues that even our experience of nature points to the creative energy and purpose of the Infinite.

10. Steve McIntosh, in *The Presence of the Infinite: The Spiritual Experience of Beauty, Truth, and Goodness*, underlines how the Infinite One has made the experience of these qualities available. Experience points to the reality of Transcendence.

a *personal* God who is love and light does ring true, deep in my soul. This capacity is essential to the nature of the statements made about the kind of God in whom we believe. So a second component of the truth test is that it must have a sense of authenticity, and be congruent in my inner sense of what we believe to be the most important dimension of our understanding of God: that God is love. "God is love, and those that abide in love abide in God, and God abides in them."[11] There is truth in a logical syllogism and a statement that describes what is. Yet when speaking about God, there is the additional dimension of sensing as we believe that I have felt the presence of the God whom we partially define as being love and truth. Jesus, as the expression of God according to the author of John's Gospel, says it so clearly, that he was full of grace (love) and truth.[12] The same deep belief in the God of love is also central to Islamic understanding. On occasion, Islamic faith is stereotyped as having a concept of God who is an angry judge. Noted Islam scholar Sayyed Hossein Nasr writes: "The idea propagated by certain Western scholars and Christian apologists that the God of Islam is the God of justice but not of Mercy, Compassion, and Love is totally false. God's Mercy, Compassion, Forgiveness, and Love are mentioned more times in the Quran than are His Justice and Retribution."[13] Any belief in God that has the ring of truth for me must include the affirmation that the God we believe exists must be a God who by nature and definition is a God who loves without condition and compassionately engages in resisting harmful and negative forces, heals the sick, and cares for the needy.

A third and fourth value and belief for me to underline, if I am to continue to believe in God, is that there must be a sense that God is a God of justice, that all are treated fairly, that humans have the obligation to diligently work for a more just and humane society and world, and that this will lead to peace.[14] Two relatively recent trends in Christian theology have been of help to me, as I sense being called to join with God in eliminating human suffering and seeking a more just world. There are times when I

---

11. 1 John 4:16b.

12. John 1:14.

13. Nasr, *Heart of Islam*, 203.

14. Lingering in the background of these statements about truth, love, and justice is also the question of why, if God is all-loving, God nevertheless allows for evil and suffering. There are books on this topic as well, such as John Hick's *Evil and the God of Love*. But the reading of book by a fine scholar and person of deep integrity doesn't erase the concern. To say that God is in process and best described by liberation theology helps, but I continue to wonder.

need to just set aside the questions of why evil and suffering exist, and then to align my modest intelligence and abilities with my deep belief that we are called by God to engage in a wide range of activities that care about and attempt to remove suffering and seek to create a more just and humane social order for all people. There are times when I must say, "Mine is not to reason why, but mine is to do or die." I must engage in the task of reducing suffering and creating a just setting in which life is good and meaningful for all. I may only be able to engage is a small way, given what I am able to do, but that small task must be done.[15]

I want to underline at this point as well that peace is possible when there is justice. Peace without justice is very rare, and where there is injustice, people in time will often seek violent means of restoring justice, and the process defeats itself. The prophet Isaiah writes about justice and peace: "He [God] shall judge between the nations, and shall arbitrate for many peoples; they shall beat their swords into plowshares, and their spears into pruning hooks; nation shall not life up sword against nation, neither shall they learn war any more" (Isa 2:4).

THEN DREAM: FIND, FOLLOW, AND FINISH

So I looked for a path that would help my dream come true, that would have at its center the heartbeat of the Christian faith, the attempt to be a person for others, following the pattern of life that was lived by Jesus, yet in the contemporary world. It would be the dream that undergirds my life. Yes, I knew about some of the other dimensions of Christian faith and ministry, but at this point in my life I felt a fairly clear tug, trusting God's love and forgiveness, *to find and follow a path*, not unlike the path followed by Jesus, one that was centered in helping people heal, find their way, and live in a setting of justice and peace. It became my motivating dream. Doing so in a learning center such as a university felt like it might be a good fit for me, given my interests and yet undeveloped gifts. It was the setting in life where I had a high degree of comfort and yet challenge. There were many choices, not just two with the selection of the one not taken.

As I went through the college years, I explored a few of them, and I took into account, as far as I was able at that point, the motivation behind and the pattern of my choices. I had come from a family with some history

---

15. I read Harvard professor Michael J. Sandel's book *Justice: What's the Right Thing to Do?* and try to answer his question.

with higher education. My parents were reasonably well educated, and there was a family history of relatively successful ancestors. It was assumed that I would attend a good university, make good choices about other dimensions of life, and have a modestly good and successful life. I have followed that sense of the future for me that was present in the family, although not without struggle.

While my family was not religious, I did get involved with a church and in religious activities while I attended university, and I also continued my interest in sports. I thought about teaching and coaching, but deep within was another voice, one that sounded like a call to go into the ministry, with a special interest in working with college and university students. As I started seminary, following graduation from the university, I focused my learning on the possibility of working with students and even getting an advanced degree, beyond the Master of Divinity, that would quality me for a place in a university setting. It was a dream that was becoming a path, not always clear, but persistently present, and I thought that I had found a way that would enable me to work with students who cared about learning and spiritual formation. I have stayed with it now for over sixty years. I did find a path on which I felt a good measure of comfort and one that never ceased to be challenging in the areas of learning and ministry.

There were some very gifted and caring people who had followed this path and who became models for me. There were people of faith who were yet intellectually honest and struggled with a whole range of challenging questions. These were the years of the Vietnam War, the cultural shifts of the 1960s, the literature of existentialism, and the quest for liberation by women and people of color. These people I admired cared deeply about global problems and human suffering, had time to grapple with the profound intellectual challenges and social unrest of the era, and somehow cared enough to nurture me forward toward a career of service. They helped me find a path and then follow it with deep commitment. At that time, I begin to learn about the work of Mother Teresa, and found inspiration in the life and writing of a whole range of people who were devoted to creating a more empathic and just social system.[16] It was Mother Teresa who spoke about a path and how she found it, and then went on to describe how she followed it. She wrote:

16. I was deeply moved by the commitment and cause of Martin Luther King Jr. and the writing of Thomas Merton, and found inspiration from the life and faith of Pope John Paul II. I also immersed myself in the writing of people outside the Christian faith such as the Dalai Lama and Thich Nhat Hanh.

Remember the words of St. Matthew's Gospel:

> I was hungry and you gave me no food,
> I was thirsty and you gave me no drink,
> I was a stranger ad you did not welcome me,
> Naked and you did not clothe me,
> Sick an in prison, and you did not visit me.

> My poor ones in the world's slums are like the suffering Christ. In them God's Son lives and dies, and through them God shows me his true faith.[17]

What struck me was how she grasped so fully the gift of God's love, even though it was revealed to her in a setting where there was intense suffering. Yet it was where she found the visible expression of how Jesus lived and cared for the poor.

I was reminded that my vision for helping to relieve human suffering was sometimes almost a romantic ideal, one that I felt drawn to, but found very difficult to practice. Yet when learning about the sacrificial life of Mother Teresa, I discovered that for her it was day-to-day engagement with the poor in the setting of total poverty. I was also taken with the way she sometimes spoke about the shift in her feelings, not always full of joy, but how she remained true in her commitment to follow the path to which she had been called. I was not prepared for her path, but did sense that I might be able to follow my path, one more in keeping with my development as a more mature person. My learning from this reflection, my dream, is that we may be shown a path to follow, claim it, and commit to following it, even when it gets difficult. There were moments when I wondered if I was on the right path, whether I was being true to following my dream, and whether I might deviate from it because it was too difficult. For example, I did serve for a while in a slightly different expression of how I envisioned my path, focusing more on the administrative side and support of those on a comparable path. I did the work in a faithful way, but found less fulfillment in it, even though it was as an expression of my dream. But I did remember and take into account that following my dream would involve times of frustration and discontent. I was challenged, made a few mistakes in my work, and suffered some from these mistakes. I experienced some insecurity and there were modest failures in fulfilling my responsibilities. But I recovered and was blessed to find still another a way to work in a university setting,

---

17. Mother Teresa, *Life in the Spirit*, 1. (Matt 25:35)

Section Three: The Current Practices of Spirituality

in which I had the privilege of working with students and continuing my research and writing. I learned from my struggle to carry out the mission in a different way, though I did not do it with the ease and grace of other assignments. I was comforted, as I remembered the account of the work of Mother Teresa, that every day cannot be one of complete joy and affirmation; many days are hard work, filled with frustration, and even a sense of not serving in the best possible way. And God may seem to be very distant.

It did bring me to the third stage of my dream: I found a path, I followed the path, and I am in the process of completing my walk and finishing it with gratitude. I am in retirement, but a joyful one in which I have been able to stay on the path that has been my life journey. I have continued teaching in adult education in several churches, and with a less demanding schedule I have been able to continue my research and writing. If my path was to learn and teach, I am now at the stage at which I finish the journey, still involved in some teaching and writing, but aware of aging. I find wisdom and comfort as I read about the last days of Mother Teresa. While ill and in bed in the evening of September 5, 1997, in Calcutta, she had trouble breathing. The story goes on:

> Unexpectedly the electricity failed and the whole house was in darkness. Foreseeing an emergency, the sisters had secured two independent electric supplies. But both lines went out at the same time; such a thing had never happened before. Prompt and expert medical aid could not help, as the breathing machine (Bi-PAP) could not be started. It was 9:30 P.M. While Calcutta was in darkness, the earthly life of the one who brought so much light to this city and to the whole world was extinguished. Even so, her mission continues: from heaven she still responds to Jesus' call, "Come, be My light."[18]

Find your path; follow your dream; finish your life's goals.

---

18. Kolodiejchuk, *Mother Teresa: Come Be My Light*, 333.

Bibliography

Allen, Diogenes. *The Traces of God.* Cambridge, MA: Cowley, 1981.
Armstrong, Karen. *The Case for God.* New York: Knopf, 2009.
Aslan, Reza. *No god But God.* New York: Random House, 2006.
Bloom, Howard. *The God Problem: How a Godless Cosmos Creates.* Amherst, NY: Prometheus, 2012.
Bonhoeffer, Dietrich. *Letters and Papers from Prison.* Minneapolis: Fortress, 2015.
Carmody, Denise L., and John T. Carmody. *Ways to the Center: An Introduction to World Religions.* Belmont, CA: Wadsworth, 1984.
Chödrön, Pema. *No Time to Lose: A Timely Guide to the Way of the Bodhisattva.* Boston: Shambhala, 2005.
Cohen, Andrew. *Evolutionary Enlightenment: A New Path to Spiritual Awakening.* New York: SelectBooks, 2011.
Condemi, Silvana, and Francois Savatier. *A Pocket History of Human Evolution.* New York: The Experiment, 2019.
Curry, Michael. *Love Is the Way.* New York: Penguin Random House, 2020.
Dalai Lama. *Ethics for the New Millennium.* New York: Riverhead, 1998.
Dalai Lama, and Howard C. Cutler. *The Art of Happiness: A Handbook for Living.* New York: Riverhead, 1998.
Das, Lama Surya. *Awakening the Buddha Within.* New York: Bantam, 1997.
Dawkins, Richard. *The God Delusion,* Boston: Houghton Mifflin, 2006.
Delio, Ilia. *The Birth of the Dancing Star: My Journey from Cradle Catholic to Cyborg Christian.* Maryknoll, NY: Orbis, 2019.
———. *The Emergent Christ: Exploring the Meaning of Catholic in an Evolutionary Universe.* Maryknoll, NY: Orbis, 2011.
———. *Making All Things New.* Maryknoll, NY: Orbis, 2015.

Bibliography

———. *The Unbearable Wholeness of Being*. Maryknoll, NY: Orbis, 2015.
Easwaran, Eknath. *Introduction and Translation*. Tomales, CA: Nilgiri, 2007.
Esposito, John L., *Islam: The Straight Path*. 3rd ed. New York: Oxford University Press, 2005.
Ferguson, Duncan. *Exploring the Spirituality of the World Religions: The Quest for Personal, Spiritual, and Social Transformation*. New York: Continuum, 2010.
———. *Lovescapes: Mapping the Geography of Love*. Eugene, OR: Cascade, 2012.
———. *Mindful Spirituality: The Intentional Cultivation of the Spiritual Life: A Book of Daily Readings*. Eugene, OR: Wipf & Stock, 2018.
Fox, Matthew. *The Coming of the Cosmic Christ*. San Francisco: HarperOne, 1988.
———. *Creation Spirituality: Liberating Gifts for the Peoples of the Earth*. San Francisco: HarperSanFrancisco, 1991.
———. *Original Blessing: A Primer in Creation Spirituality*. New York: Penguin, 2000.
Garrett, Greg, and Sabrina Fountain. *The Courage to See*. Louisville: Westminster John Knox Press, 2019.
Hall, Sid. "Creation Spirituality: The Six Essentials." AllCreation.org, July 2019. http://www.allcreation.org/home/cs-6.
Hanh, Thich Nhat. *How to Love*. Berkeley, CA: Parallax, 2014.
———. *Teachings on Love*. Berkeley, CA: Parallax, 1997.
Harris, Sam. *The End of Faith*. New York: Norton, 2005.
Hitchens, Christopher. *god Is Not Great: How Religion Poisons Everything*. New York: Twelve: Hachette, 2007.
Jayne, Julian. *Origins of Consciousness and the Breakdown of the Bicameral Mind*. New York: Houghton Mifflin, 1976.
Klostermaier, Klause. *A Short History of Hinduism*. London: One World, 2000.
Kung, Hans. *Does God Exist?: An Answer for Today*. Translated by Edward Quinn. Garden City, NY: 1980.
Lane, Beldan C. *Backpacking with the Saints*. New York: Oxford University Press, 2014
———. *The Great Conversation: The Nurture and Care of the Soul*. New York: Oxford University Press, 2019.
L'Engle, Madeleine. *The Irrational Season*. New York: Seabury, 1997.
Mafi, Maryam, trans. *Rumi Day by Day*. Charlottesville, VA: Hampton Roads, 2014.
McIntosh, Steve. *The Presence of the Infinite: The Spiritual Experience of Beauty, Truth, and Goodness*. Wheaton IL: Theosophical, 2015.
Mother Teresa. *Life in the Spirit: Reflections, Meditations, Prayers*. Edited by Kathryn Spink. San Francisco: Harper & Row, 1983.
———. *Mother Teresa: Come Be My Light*. Edited by Brian Kolodiejchuk. New York: Image Doubleday, 2007.
Nasr, Seyyed Hossein. *The Heart of Islam*. San Francisco: HarprerSanFrancisco, 2002.
Pelikan, Jaroslav. *Christian Doctrine and Modern Culture (Since 1700)*. Vol. 5 of *The Christian Tradition: A History of the Development of Doctrine* . Chicago: University of Chicago Press, 1971–1989.
Pinkar, Steven. *Enlightenment Now: The Case for Reason, Science, Humanism, and Progress*. New York: Penguin Random House, 2018.
Placher, William C. *The Domestication of Transcendence: How Modern Thinking about God Went Wrong*. Louisville: Westminster John Knox Press, 1996.
Richardson, Heather Cox. *Letters from an American*, June 1, 2021. https://heathercoxrichardson.substack.com/p/june-1-2021.

Bibliography

Schott, Hanna. *Love in a Time of Hate*. Harrisonburg, VA: Herald, 2017.
Seddon, Mohammad, and Raana Bokhar. *The Illustrated Encyclopedia of Islam*. London: Lorenz, 2009.
Swineburn, Richard. *The Coherence of Theism*. Oxford: Oxford University Press, 2016.
Teilhard de Chardin, Pierre. *The Divine Milieu*. New York: Harper Torchbooks, 1957.
———. *The Future of Man*. New York: Harper & Row, 1959.
———. *The Phenomenon of Man*. London: Collins, 1955.
Tillich, Paul. *The Courage to Be*. New Haven, CT: Yale University Press, 1961.
Wilson, E. O. *The Meaning of Human Existence*. New York: Norton, 2010.

Index

Abraham, background of, 54, 108
Abrahamic monotheistic religions, 4, 11, 52
Abu Bakr, 115
Africa
    Homo sapiens evolutionary development, 21
    prehistoric culture, 29–31
ahimsa (nonviolence), 102
al Qaeda, 127–28
Al-Adawiyyah, Rabiah, 119
Alaska Native people, 13–14
Alexander, Cecil Frances, 74n5
"All Things Bright and Beautiful" (hymn), 74
Allah, 60, 113, 117
almsgiving, 61, 114
American Indians, prehistoric culture, 26–29
Anselm, 70
The Appearance of Man (Teilhard), 80
The Art of Happiness: A Handbook for Living (Dalai Lama & Cutler), 87–88
artificial intelligence (AI), 82

Ashkenazi Jews, 107
atman, 42, 102
atonement, doctrine of, 70–71
Augustine, 70
Aurobindo, Sri (Ghose), 98–100
Australia, prehistoric culture, 29–31
autocratic governments, 133, 134

Bakr, Abu, 115
Being Peace (Hahn), 95
Bhagavad Gita, 42, 98
bhakti, 101–2
Bible
    creation story, 69–70, 80
    Hebrew bible, 56, 112
    as model of cultural change, 14–16
    New Testament, 59
    preunderstanding of, 139n3
blessings, 74–75
Bo (Bodhi or enlightenment), 45
Bodhisattva, 63
Brahman (Transcendence), 43, 98
Brahmin class, 42, 44
Buber, Martin, 109
Buddha, 44, 96

Index

Buddhism, 44–48, 85–87
Bultmann, Rudolf, 139n3
Bush, George W., 128

caliphs (Islamic practice), 115
Calvin, John, 70, 71, 74
Carmody, Denise L., 22
Carmody, John T., 22
case study, Alaska Natives, 13–14
ceremonies, development of, 27–28
Chödrön, Pema, 63, 86, 95–97
Christianity
    apostle Paul and, 109
    diversity of, 115
    modification of beliefs, 137–38
    Nehru's influence, 101
    personal Transcendence, 115
    population size, 113
    premodern, 57–59
    question of true religion, 77
    world-wide spread of, 61
Christopher, David, 151n9
Churchill, Winston, 101
class system (*varna*), 102–3
Cohen, Andrew, 3n1
Comfortable with Uncertainty (Chödrön), 96
committed spirituality
    Islam, 59–61, 112–19
    Judaism, 54–57, 106–12
    overview, 104–6
communities, formation of, 37
compassion, 75, 76, 90
The Compassionate Box (Chödrön), 96
compassionate spirituality
    earth charter, 125–34
    inherent transcendence, 123–25
Confessions (Augustine), 70
conflict, 137–42
consciousness
    development of, 21n2
    level of, 66
    state of, 88
Conservative Judaism, 107
contemplation. *See* inward view
contemplative spirituality
    Aurobindo, Sri (Ghose), 98–100

    Buddhism and, 44–48, 85–87
    Chödrön, Pema, 95–97
    Dalai Lama, 87–93
    Gandhi, Mahatma, 66, 97, 100–103
    Hinduism, 97–98
    inward turning, 84–85
    Thich Nhat Hanh, 8, 85–86, 93–95, 154n16
cosmic evolutionary pattern, 3
cosmic transcendent other, 9
creation spirituality
    components of, 72–78
    historical roots, 69–72
    overview, 65–69
    science/religion integration, 79
    as a spiritual movement, 68–69
    Teilhard's thought on, 79–80
"Creation Spirituality: The Six Essentials" (Hall), 74
cultural norms
    biblical model, 14–16
    patterns of change, 13–14
Cutler, Howard C., 87–89

Dalai Lama, 8, 85, 87–93, 154n16
Damaris, 16
Darwin, Charles, 89, 98, 99
Dawkins, Richard, 124, 150
Delio, Ilia, 8, 81–83, 85
democratic form of government, 132–34
devas, term usage, 41
Dhammapada, 42
dharma, 43, 44, 88–89, 96
din, term usage, 114
Dionysius, 14–15
diversity
    of Alaska Natives, 13
    in the ancient world, 31
    of beliefs, 145–46
    within the Cosmos, 76–77
    within Islam, 115–16
    within Judaism, 106–8
Divine, term usage, 9–10, 67
The Divine Milieu (Teilhard), 80
dukka (suffering), 45

The Earth Charter (UNESCO), 125–34

Index

East Asia, 36, 45
ecological integrity, 130–31
ecological justice, 73
economic justice, 131–33
Eightfold Path, 46–47, 86, 96
Einstein, Albert, 12, 111, 139, 151
Elohim, 55n6
The Emergent Universe: Exploring the Meaning of Catholic in an Evolutionary Universe (Delio), 82
Enlightenment era, 7–8m4, 79–80
environment concerns. *See* compassionate spirituality
Eskimos, prehistoric culture, 26–29
Essenes, 109
eternal life, concept of, 28
Ethics for the New Millennium (Dalai Lama), 92
European culture, 30
Evil and the God of Love (Hick), 152n14
evolution
    evolutionary cosmic pattern, 3
    'the fall' as name for, 70
    Homo sapiens development, 21, 21n1, 81
evolutionary accelerator, 29n9
Evolutionary Enlightenment (Cohen), 3n1
exclusive component of religions, 77–78
The Experience of God: Being, Consciousness, Bliss (Hart), 150, 151

faith
    dimensions of, 53
    meaning in life and, 4
    term usage, 52–53
faithfulness, ways of. *See* committed spirituality; upward view
fall/redemption paradigm, 72–73
fasting, 61
fear, omnipresence of, 34–35
five mindfulness trainings, 94–95
Five Pillars of Islam, 61, 114
foundational literature. *See* Bible; Quran; Upanishads
Four Immeasurable Minds, 93–94
Four Nobel Truths, 46, 86

Four Passing Sights, 44
four-caste system, 42–43
Fox, Matthew, 72, 74, 85, 105
Francis, Saint, 66
Free Church tradition, 71
free will, predestination and, 71
Freud, Sigmund, 89

Gabriel, archangel, 113
Gandhi, Mohandas "Mahatma," 66, 97, 100–103
Ginsburg, Ruth Bader, 56
global catastrophic risks to human family, 126–27
global problems, 78
God
    Allah, 60, 113, 117
    creation spirituality and, 65–68
    Elohim, 55n6
    existence of, 149–51
    goodness without, 38–40
    as love, 152, 152n14
    Paul's insights, 16, 19
    revelation from, 50
    suffering and, 152–53
    as Supreme Spirit, 28
    understanding of, 8–10
    Yahweh, 55–56
God in Search of Man and *Man Is Not Alone* (Heschel), 110
Great Britain, Stonehenge, 25
Great Renunciation, 44

Hajj (Islamic practice), 61, 114
Hall, Sid, 74, 78
Hanh, Thich Nhat. *See* Thich Nhat Hanh
happiness, 87–89
Harris, Sam, 150
Hart, David Bentley, 150, 151
heaven, 67
Hebrew bible, 56, 112
Hebrew people. *See* Judaism
Hegel, G.W.F., 98, 99
Heschel, Abraham, 109–10
Hick, John, 152n14
Hinduism, 40–43, 97–98

Index

history
    creation spirituality, 69–72
    nature and, 21–23
    See also prehistoric cultures
Hitler, Adolf, 107–8, 148
Holocaust story, 39, 107, 110
The Holy Universe (Christopher), 151n9
hominids, varieties of, 23
Homo sapiens
    development stages of, 22–23
    evolutionary development, 21, 21n1
    forces in nature and, 24
    needs of, 23–24
    religious impulses, 24–25
Hopi culture, 28
How to Love (Hahn), 95n8
human consciousness, 10, 31, 37, 138, 151
human development, stages of, 22–23, 81
human life, nature of, 45
Hume, David, 89

I and Thou (Buber), 109
imam, term usage, 115n8
immanence, term usage, 5
India
    Aryan population, influence in, 42
    Aurobindo, Sri (Ghose), 98–100
    Buddhism and, 44–48, 85–87
    Gandhi, 66, 97, 100–103
    Hinduism and, 40–43, 97–98
    Pakistan and, 101, 101n14
Indra, Hindu god, 42
inherent transcendence, 123–25
integration process, 147–49
introspection. *See* contemplative spirituality
inward view
    Buddhism, 44–48, 85–87
    Hinduism, 40–43, 97–98
    overview, 36–40, 84–85
    Islam, 59–61, 112–19, 152

Jalal-Ud-Din Rumi, 118
Jesus, 57–59, 57n7, 66, 68–71
jihad, term usage, 61, 114
John Paul II, Pope, 154n16

Judaism, 54–57, 106–12
justice, 78, 131–33, 152–53
Justice: What's the Right Thing to Do? (Sandel), 153n15

Kant, Immanuel, 5, 82, 98
karma-samsara, term usage, 42, 46
kauna (compassion), 45, 93
Khadija (wife of Muhammad), 113
Kierkegaard, Søren, 53
King, Martin Luther, Jr., 102, 154n16
Kornfield, Jack, 121
Küng, Hans, 150

liberation theology, 152n14
The Life Divine (Aurobindo), 98
life-denying characteristics, 7–8
life-giving characteristics, 6
love, 81–82, 89, 93–95, 152
Luther, Martin, 71

maîtiri [metta] (lovingkindness), 93
Making All Things New: Catholicity, Cosmology, Consciousness (Delio), 82
Mathnawi (Rumi), 118–19
McIntosh, Steve, 151n10
The Meaning of Human Existence (Wilson), 125
medicine man, 31
meditation
    link with God, 9
    Moses and, 55
    Muhammad and, 60, 67
    nature and, 32, 52
    See also contemplative spirituality; inward view
Meir, Golda, 56
Merton, Thomas, 154n16
metta [maîtiri] (lovingkindness), 45
Middle East, 36, 57, 113
Mindful Spirituality (Ferguson), 50
mindfulness trainings, 94–95
miracles, term usage, 67
moksha, 42, 43, 102
Monk, William Henry, 74n5

Morality: Restoring the Common Good in Divided Times (Sachs), 111
Moses, 55, 66
mosque, 114
Mr. Rogers (television show), 74
mudita (gentleness, joy), 45, 94
mudita (joy), 94
Muhammad, 60–61, 66, 113–15, 118
Muslim people. *See* Islam
Mwari, hymn to, 29–30
mystic, capacity to be, 76
mystical paths, 75–76
myth, term usage, 29

Nasr, Sayyed Hossein, 152
nature
    ancient world and, 32–33
    history and, 21–23
    religion and, 23–25
Nehru, 101
neoliberal Christians, 59n9
New Testament, 59
New Zealand, 133
nirvana, 45
No Time to Lose: The Way of the Bodhisattva (Chödrön), 95–96
nonviolence (*ahimsa*), 102
noosphere, term usage, 81

Obama, Barack, 128
obedience, ways of. *See* committed spirituality; upward view
Omega Point, 81, 98, 105
Original Blessing (Fox), 72, 74
original sin, doctrine of, 70
Orthodox Christian tradition, 71
Orthodox Judaism, 107, 111
outward extension
    history, and nature, 21–23
    prehistoric cultures, 26–31
    preliterate people's religions, 26
    religion, and nature, 23–25
    themes and practices, 31–35

Pakistan, 101, 101n14
Palestine, 111
panentheism, term usage, 9, 67

pantheism, 67
Parousia (Second Coming), 81
patterns
    cosmic evolutionary, 3, 81
    cultural norms, 13–14
    of religious life, 35
    transcendence design and structure, 3
Paul, Apostle, 14–16, 17n12, 19, 58
peace, nature of, 95
personal Transcendence, 3–4
Pharisees, 109
The Phenomenon of Man (Teilhard), 80
Pinker, Steven, 38
The Places that Scare You (Chödrön) 96
Plato, 12, 98, 99, 148
Polynesian culture, 30
practices, of beliefs, 146
predestination, human free will and, 71
prehistoric cultures
    Africa and Australia, 29–31
    American Indians and Eskimos, 26–29
preliterate people's religions, 26
premodern world
    inward view (*See* inward view)
    outward view (*See* outward extension)
    upward view (*See* upward view)
The Presence of the Infinite (McIntosh), 151n10
present moment, focus on, 33–34
preunderstanding, 139n3
progressive Christians, 59n9
protective elements, 34–35
Protestant Christian tradition, 71
Pueblo culture, 28
Putin, Vladimir, 133

Quran, 60, 113, 115

Ramadan (Islamic practice), 61, 114
reason, ways of. *See* creation spirituality
Recitation (Quran), 113
reflection, ways of. *See* creation spirituality
Reform Judaism, 107
Reformation era, 70
reincarnation, 28

Index

relationships, importance of, 89–90
religion
    definition of, 5
    nature and, 23–25
religious leaders, vocation and, 7
resources, efficient distribution of, 132
revelation, from God, 50
Richardson, Heather Cox, 133
rituals, development of, 27–28
Roman Catholic Church, 71, 80, 82, 118
Rumi, 50
Rumi, Jalal-Ud-Din, 118–19
Russian Orthodox tradition, 14

Sachs, Jonathan, 111
Sadducees, 109
Sakat (Islamic practice), 61, 114
Salat (Islamic practice), 61, 114
samsara, 97, 102
Sandel, Michael J., 153n15
sangha (community), 96
satya (truth), 102
satyagraha (truth-force), 102
Saudi Arabia, 113
science
    Enlightenment era, 79–80
    religion integration, 79
    theology and, 38
Second Coming (*Parousia*), 81
secular Judaism, 107
self-realization, 37
Sephardim Jews, 107
September 11, 2001 attack, 127–28
Shahadah (Islamic practice), 61, 114
shamans, 25, 28, 31
Shantideva (Indian sage), 63, 96
shariah (law), 114, 115
Shia (Islamic group), 115, 116
Siddhartha Gautama, 44–45
sidq, term usage, 119
sin, doctrine of, 70
social justice, 78, 131–33
souls of ancestors, 30
South Asia, 36, 103, 113
spiritual liberation, 47–48
spiritual pathways
    choices, 135–37, 153–56

    conflict and, 137–42
    diversity, 145–46
    foundations of, 149–53
    integration process, 147–49, 150
    life-denying characteristics, 7–8
    life-giving characteristics, 6
    practices, 146
    selection, 144–47
    six essentials, 74–78
    understanding, 142–44, 146–47
stages of life, Hinduism and, 42
Stonehenge, Great Britain, 25
suffering
    Buddhist teaching on, 45–46, 90–91, 94–95
    God and, 152–53
    transcendence in, 39–40, 145
    ways of relieving, 154–56
Sufism (Islamic mysticism), 118–19
Sunni (Islamic group), 115, 116
Supermind/Spirit, 98
Surya Das, Lama, 48
Sutras, term usage, 42
Swinburne, Richard, 150

taboos, 29
Talmud, 110
tanha (craving), 45–46
Teachings of Love, 93–94
Teilhard de Chardin, Pierre, 8, 79–81, 85, 98, 99, 105
Teresa, Mother, 66, 154–56
theism, 67
themes and practices, 31–35
theology, science and, 38
Thich Nhat Hanh, 8, 85–86, 93–95, 154n16
Thomas Aquinas, 71
"Three Jewels of Buddhism," 96
Torah, 56, 110
totems, term usage, 31
traffic accident scenario, 38–39
transcendence/Transcendence
    challenges in understanding of, 8–10
    change and commitment, 17–18
    choices, in times of great change, 11–12

Index

disbelief in, 145–47
going forward, 11
historical model, 14–16
inherent transcendence, 123–25
overview, 3–8, 51–52
term usage, 4–6, 4n2, 135–37
transcendental monism, 36
Trump, Donald, 128
Trump administration, 133
truth, 102, 149
truth-force (*satyagraha*), 102

ummah (community of faith believers), 60, 113, 114
The Unbearable Wholeness of Being: God, Evolution and the Power of Love (Delio), 81–82
understanding, 142–44, 146–47
UNESCO (United Nations Educational, Scientific and Cultural Organization), 125–34
United Nations, 126, 134
universal values, implementing. *See* compassionate spirituality
Upanishads, 37, 41–42, 43, 98
upekkha [upeksha] (equanimity), 45, 94
upward view
    Islam, 59–61, 112–19
    Judaism, 54–57, 106–12
    overview, 49–53

values, 5, 51, 89, 92–93, 149–53
varna (class system), 102–3
Varuna, Hindu god, 42
Vedas, 41–42, 99
violence, elimination of, 133
vision quest, 28
vocations, of religious leaders, 15–16

The Way of the Bodhisattva (Shantideva), 96
wealth, equitable distribution of, 132
When Things Fall Apart (Chödrön), 96
Wilbur, Ken, 12n11, 99, 150n6
Wilson, Edward O., 12, 124
The Wisdom of No Escape, Start Where You Are (Chödrön), 95–96
women
    Buddhist teachings and, 95–97
    gifts of discernment and wisdom, 31n11
    Judaism and, 56
    role in guiding faith followers, 52n2
World Economic Forum, 127

Yahweh, 55–56

Zealots, 109
Zimbabwe, 29–30

www.ingramcontent.com/pod-product-compliance
Lightning Source LLC
Chambersburg PA
CBHW070918180426
43192CB00038B/1751